THE
HOUSE
WELCOME HOME!

The House Welcome Home!
Copyright © 2013 by Marco A. Peixoto
ISBN: 978-0-98848991-2
Library of Congress Control Number: 2012951539
English Version - First Edition
Printed in the United States of America

2 4 6 8 10 9 7 5 3 1

Cover design & layout by Bryan Reed of liquid$_2$ Design – www.liquid2.com
Edited by Duane A. Brown
English translation by: Pastor Jim Pope, Pink Hill, North Carolina
Photo Mosaic - Epicentro Collection

Translated from Portuguese version:
Copyright 2011 by Marco Antonio Rodrigues Peixoto
Epicentro
Praia do Flamengo, 72-A, Rio de Janeiro-RJ - Brazil
Tel 55 21 3506-1900 - Cep 22210-030
www.comunidadezonasul.com.br

Except where noted otherwise, all Biblical citations have been extracted from the Biblia Sagrada Versao Almeida Revista e Atualizada, SBB.

Published by
Cranberry Quill Publishing, Inc.
111 Lamon Street, Suite 201, Fayetteville, NC 28301
www.CranberryQuill.com

Dedication

I would like to thank the entire ministry team at Comunidale Evangélica International da Zona Sul: pastors, deacons and staff, along with the entire church, for their love and dedication to THE HOUSE, as well as for their commitment and support.

And, especially, my dear wife and my precious daughters, who dedicate their lives to THE HOUSE, and are a living expression of everything I have learned from God.

Together we will impact this generation through a lifestyle
that declares that JESUS CHRIST IS LORD.

CONTENTS

Introduction

"One thing I ask from the Lord, this only do I seek: that I may dwell in the house of the Lord all the days of my life"
Psalms 27:4

The central theme of this book is THE HOUSE, meaning the church of the Living God. We will discuss different aspects of this HOUSE and what we should find within it.

It is fundamental that we understand the importance of the House of God, especially at a time when many Christians who love God are not planted in a local church.

God has great things to do through your church! Be a part of God's plans and projects.

Keep an open mind, while reading this book, to truly understand the need to value and love the HOUSE. Remember: Whoever loves the HOUSE loves the God of the HOUSE.

Believe, and we will see signs and wonders through a church that expresses extraordinary faith in Jesus.

Come be planted and bear fruit! WELCOME HOME!

CHAPTER 1
The Father moves quickly!

MARCO A. PEIXOTO

But the father said to his servants, "Quick! Bring the best robe and put it on him.
Put a ring on his finger and sandals on his feet."
Luke 15:22

In modern days, the words "quick" and "hurry" are well known and used by all of us. We are driven by an urgency which rules our era, where people are always rushing, and therefore this verse in Luke may not have gotten our attention. However, upon studying the Bible, we see that things were not like this in Jesus' time.

This was a time when there were no cell phones, overnight mail or internet, when most people walked to get anywhere and had to wait, with plenty of patience, for the arrival of a relative or news. In fact, the Bible mentions "quick" or "hurry" very few times. In the current Almeida version of the Bible in Portuguese, published by the Brazilian Biblical Society, there are about thirty references in the Old Testament and only about ten in the New Testament. Jesus himself used these words few times, one of which was when he said to Zacchaeus, "*Come down immediately. I must stay at your house today."* (Luke 19:5)

However, when we look at the life of Jesus, His teachings to the disciples and the actions of the Holy Spirit propelled the church in the book of Acts, we can see that God moves "quickly"! Not the kind of "quickly" that makes us cut into the middle of a line or push someone out of the way to be first, or honk in traffic all the time, but to act quickly in our own lives to respond to His urgency that we be transformed into His likeness. Everything that God wants to do in our lives, He wants done quickly! We are the ones who "hold up the line" with our slowness, but God moves quickly!

In Luke 15 we find the well-known parable of the prodigal son, in this parable the father of the prodigal son symbolizes God. We know that Jesus used symbolism in His parables to communicate principles of the Kingdom of God to His listeners. In this particular parable, God is represented by the father figure, who was home awaiting his son's return – the son who had spent his entire inheritance on a dissolute lifestyle.

Before returning to his father's house, the son had reached the point of starvation, with no one to give him anything to eat. After losing his wealth, he had been abandoned by his fickle friends. He had finally been given a job caring for pigs, in a place far from his home. But the story says that one day this young man got up, sorry for what he had done, and decided to return to his father. He returned to his father repentant.

After making the mistake of leaving his father's house, the young man does everything in the right order: first he got up; next he repented and returned to his father. However, there is something wrong with this young man. Wrong? But he did everything right, pastor! *He repented and returned home; isn't that what God, the Father, is waiting for us to do?* Let's look at the father – God – in the story and see the warning He gives us through the example of the prodigal son.

THE HOUSE | WELCOME HOME!

When the son returns home, his father sees him first. And as soon as he sees him from afar, he runs to him and embraces him. If you are a father, you know how it feels to hug your child after a long time away. Maybe a business trip has kept you apart; or your tight schedule prevents you from seeing him often enough; or maybe he went on vacation with his grandparents in another city. The only thing you want is to hug your child. And if you are a son, you also know how it feels to be embraced. A hug means affection and caring, but in this parable, there is also another meaning. At that time, by law, any son who embarrassed his father through wrong-doing should be stoned to death. In this parable, however, the father embraced his son. This embrace meant protection. The father covered his son and granted him his forgiveness.

At that moment, everything unfolds in a special way: the son, repentant, returns to his father's house; the father kisses and hugs him; until the son stops him to make a statement. Let's take a look at the story at this point:

> So he got up and went to his father. But while he was still a long way off, his father saw him and was filled with compassion for him; he ran to his son, threw his arms around him and kissed him. The son said to him, "Father, I have sinned against heaven and against you. I am no longer worthy to be called your son."
> Luke 15:20-21

When the son makes this statement, the father interrupts him and gives an order:

> But the father said to his servants, "Quick! Bring the best robe and put it on him. Put a ring on his finger and sandals on his feet."
> Luke 15:22

Note that the father did not say: "Bring the best robe for my son". He said, "Quick! Bring the best robe." The father moves quickly. Why does he use this expression? In the Bible, there are words which, despite being small, jump out at us – and they are not there by chance. Every word in the Bible is the living Word of God! Every word, no matter how small, has a meaning and purpose. If the father in the parable wanted this to be done quickly, there was a reason for it. As I have said, the father in this story represents God, so God must move quickly! God wants to do some things quickly. What kind of things?

In the parable, the father of the young man acted quickly simply because he did not want to wait any longer to put a new robe on his son. Although the principles are correct (the son was repentant and returned to his father's house), his father was in a hurry to see him in a new robe, so he said, "Quick! Bring the best robe". However, could it be that the father just wanted his son to look better with a new robe? In fact, when analyzing the original Biblical text, we see that the robe was not just an ordinary piece of clothing. The actual translation of the original word is *robe of a prince*, special clothing.

MARCO A. PEIXOTO

Wearing a special robe

We need to get used to being in the Father's house wearing clothes that are pleasing to Him. This means we should meditate on how we present ourselves before God in our daily lives. Not to say we need to buy new pants, shirts or dresses to wear in the house of God. Wearing clothes that are pleasing to Him means behaving in a way that pleases Him and that shows we are truly His children. God is not interested in the brands of our clothing, He wants our hearts.

> *My son, give me your heart and let your eyes delight in my ways.*
> Proverbs 23:26

That special robe that the prodigal son received from his father symbolized honor, recognition and exaltation. There was only one desire in the heart of the father after embracing and kissing his son: to see him dressed appropriately; to see him dressed according to the standards of the Father; to see him dressed like royalty!

We are the people of God, washed and redeemed by the blood of the Lamb, Jesus Christ. We were bought at high price! We are not in the church to fulfill a ritual or follow a law. We are not in the church because we are being forced or because we fear the Lord's judgment against us if we are not. We are in the Father's House because we love Him! We are a part of the church because we belong to a royal family, and therefore, we wear a royal robe. We are in the church because we feel the presence, grace and love of the Father upon us. And these are the very things the world needs to see in the church. We must "wear our royal robe" so the world can see that we are God's children. Do not just take the first two steps like the prodigal son – repenting and returning to his father. If we are His children, the Father wants to see us in new a new robe, living a new life, with a new attitude. The Bible says in Romans 8:19: *"For the creation waits in eager expectation for the children of God to be revealed."*

The world is waiting for the children of God to reveal themselves, so it needs to see much more than just words. People need to see through our actions that we are children of God, people who have **returned Home** – not people in strange clothing, speaking a mystical or religious dialect! They need to see life-giving attitudes from a people who are wearing a new robe.

No matter what your cultural, social or economic standing is, we are all unified by the blood of the Lamb. When we return Home, we will receive a new robe. We all need to understand and accept this new robe from the Lord. We are princes and princesses, that is, we are royalty! This is how the devil should see and respect the people of God! The problem is when we do not realize what is rightfully ours, because we do not know the Word of God, it keeps us from fully receiving what is rightfully ours.

"Quick! Bring the best robe." The Father is saying "quick" so whoever is repenting will not have time to assume another identity except that of a child of God – heir of all His promises. The son had taken all the right steps in reconciling with his father, but he forgot the important principle of identity: *"Father, I have sinned against heaven and against you. I am no longer worthy to be called your son"* (Luke 15:21). The father interrupted him immediately so he wouldn't have time to reject what had been given him.

Let's together imagine this scene: the son returns to his father's house, broken and repentant. The father embraces him. The son is surprised because he didn't expect his Father would even see him. Being embraced and kissed by his father was already much more than he had expected. At that moment, the son declares, *"I am no longer worthy to be called your son."* And when he continues, *"So treat me like one of your help"*, the father does not give him time to continue further. He interrupts him, saying, *"Bring the best robe and put it on him"* (Luke 15:22). In other words, the father is saying, "Put a robe on him immediately, before anymore time goes by with him wearing inadequate clothing. Within my son's heart there is already brokenness and repentance; he has returned home. What else do I need? Put a robe on him quickly."

There are believers who do not enjoy what is rightfully theirs. They are satisfied with only salvation and do not know their rights as heirs. They tell themselves: I am humble, I am glad I am saved. I do not desire a car, a house, or big things in life because I am very simple. In the name of humility, we are throwing away rights that the Father has won for us through the blood of Jesus. That is what the prodigal son was doing. He wanted to be in his father's house, but not as his son. For him, earning what the servants made and eating the same food they ate was enough. Why do so many Christians prefer to live as servants in their Father's house?

Distant from the Father

Not long after that, the younger son got together all he had, set off for a distant country…
Luke 15:13

The word "distant" can refer to geographical distance or physical space; but in this parable, it means much more than that. The son distanced himself from his father – meaning he was far from the will of God, and this is the worst kind of distance for the human spirit. While he was in that distant land, a spirit of poverty took over the prodigal son. While he lived among the pigs, he acquired a new identity, personality and vision.

He had left his father's house, where he had a right to everything, took his inheritance and wandered the world, enjoying its pleasures: *"…and there wasted his possessions with prodigal living."* The New International Version of the Bible says: *"…and there squandered his wealth in wild living."* He lived recklessly. If we apply this parable today, we can imagine the young man spent all his money on all-night partying and orgies. But the main issue is not just the fact that he spent everything on orgies and parties. The issue was the young man's involvement in the world he lived in.

When he returns home to his father, his spirit is in poor condition. Why? Is it because he felt unworthy? Is it because he had spent his money on orgies? No. Those were not the main reasons for his misery. His misery came when he was living among the pigs (which really represent demons), then and there his mind and heart were changed.

In the Father's house there is protection. When we live with the Lord, we are protected by His Word, but when we walk away from His house, the spirit of this world tries to deceive us. Do not think that if you live far from God, you will maintain the same faith. Do not think that if you live far from God, you will continue speaking the language of faith. It will not happen, and the prodigal son is proof of it. He made a serious mistake by wasting his inheritance, but that's not all. By getting involved in the evil of this world and living among pigs and demons, his identity was destroyed. So when he returns home, he denies his identity saying, *"I am no longer worthy."*

But there is still another character in this story, the older brother. Although he had remained in his father's house, he also had the spirit of poverty. He did not rejoice with the return of his lost brother. He refused to celebrate. He felt unfairly treated or wronged and ignored or despised. The spirit of envy took over his heart and he was outside during the party. If you do not want to be "outside during the party", enjoy everything the Lord has prepared for you and do not waste His blessings.

Besides everything that happened that day, the father sought out his oldest son to try and convince him to join the festivities. But when he tried to talk to him, the son became outraged at his father! Being poor does not mean having little money; poverty is a bitter, jealous, greedy, petty spirit, that does not allow us to enjoy life.

There is a very important lesson in this parable that we need to consider in our lives as believers: the eldest son was living inside the house. He did not leave like the prodigal son. He did not spend any money, although he had the right to a double portion for being the oldest son. He inherited 2/3 of his father's wealth while the younger son had only 1/3. Still, he had not spent anything.

Even though the older son did not go to parties and orgies, his condition was worse than his brother's for one reason: he did not have a broken heart. He confronted his father and scolded him for his reaction to his youngest son.

The eldest son symbolizes the believer who is in church challenging God. They say to God: "I don't

THE HOUSE | WELCOME HOME!

understand. Lord, You've had so much time to solve this, why don't you just fix it? If You don't do something soon, You will never see me here again. Do You have any idea how long I have been tithing? That brother over there (a new convert for whom I have even prayed) has only been here for three months and he is really happy. What about me? I am sad and bitter…but why? Why do You treat him better than you treat me?" If you can identify with the older brother, you also need to put on a new robe.

Changing your robe

Being distant from God is a miserable feeling. Although the prodigal son had done everything correctly by repenting and returning in brokenness to his father's house, there was one principle that he did not understand. He did not realize that something was missing from his life. The mind of that young man had been limited by the evil of this world; it had been diminished by the devil. The worst part was not the sin of the flesh, but the sin in his mind.

He had spent all the money he had; committed carnal sin; he had erred! But by living within the pattern of this world, the devil polluted his mind. When he returns home, he is repentant. He weeps and is broken-hearted, but returns with a feeling of inferiority, inadequacy and guilt. *Treat me like a servant. I am unworthy of being a son.* This mentality is from Satan.

As children of God, we must understand that it is not enough to just be in the House and repentant. It is necessary to enjoy and experience the whole "package deal" that God offers us. I'm not referring to financial benefits specifically. Of course God provides financial blessings to us, but I am referring to our standing with God, the prosperity we have in Him. And when I say prosperity, I mean to live well, sleep well and be at peace with everything around you or content with what you have.

Some people earn little more than minimum wage, pay their bills and debts on time, live happy and sleep peacefully. On the other hand, there are people who make tens of thousands of dollars every month, yet live in debt and can only sleep if they take medication. That is definitely not prosperity. Prosperity means knowing how to manage; it means knowing how to multiply what you are given, as told in the parable of the ten talents (Matthew 25:14-29).

When the prodigal son returned with a spirit of poverty, he was first met with the spirit of mercy. He returned with an inferior mentality. *"I am not worthy of being your son."* But the father said, *"Quick, bring him a new robe."*

The father moves quickly. He no longer wants to see his son dressed in rags; he wants his son to feel at home, in his presence, wearing a new robe. The Father does not want His children in His presence wearing dirty rags. He wants us to be dressed like royalty.

We see that when the father and son are reunited, the first thing the father says is: "Change your clothes." The father wanted to remove his son's feelings of inferiority: "I just want to live in your home; you don't have to treat me like your son". But if the son simply lives in the house without sharing in his father's royalty, there is a problem! It takes living with the Father to have a relationship with Him. We have to be able to look into His eyes, sense His smell, hug, kiss, weep, and shout! You may feel regret and want to cry, scream or lay facedown on the floor, but when you stand up, wear the right robe! The father said "quickly", because we do not have time to be in the Father's House without the right robe. In other words, we do not have time to be in our Father's House in any identity other than as His children. In the Father's House, we are His children, heirs with Christ.

Only those who wear a royal robe, the clothing of an heir, will remain in the Father's House. The word "robe" means our righteousness, our attitudes, testimony, and position. The "robe" we wear must be consistent with who we are. For example, on an airplane, the pilot's uniform is different from the flight attendants uniform; on a ship, the captain is recognized by his special uniform, and so on.

You are an heir! God wants to see us dressed according to our status, and He moves quickly. Often, we call out to God our Father when we are dressed as servants. The slaves did not wear sandals, or jewelry. They wore simple clothes and walked barefoot. The servants of the Father do not call Him Father. They serve Him, but they are not his children. When you pray to God, you must do so as a son or daughter and heir. Your Father is the Creator of heaven and earth, of your life and everything in the world. You are entitled to receive all that He has been prepared especially for you!

God was the first to dress man. Before sin, Adam and Eve were "both naked and they felt no shame" (Genesis 2:25), "but after the fall and failure of mankind, they realized they were naked and tried to cover their nakedness with fig leaves. So, the Lord God made garments from animal skins for Adam and his wife and clothed them" (Genesis 3:21). Man had failed at a seemingly simple task. God had told them: "You are free to eat from any tree in the garden; but you must not eat from the tree of the knowledge of good and evil, for when you eat from it you will certainly die" (Genesis 2:16-17).

It was a single tree that brought down mankind. One tree. But what really happened? Adam failed in his mission. By listening to his wife, Adam was silent and gave in to what she told him, eating the fruit and sinning against God.

After Adam sinned and covered himself with fig leaves in shame (Genesis 3:7), he was stripped of the glory of God. When God called to the man "Where are you?", Adam began explaining his actions saying he was afraid because he was naked. So God asked him, "Have you eaten from the tree that I commanded you not to eat from?" And Adam replied: "It...it was this woman you gave me who ate it first then gave it to me. I didn't even want any...did you not prepare her for me? She tricked me!"

Then, God covered Adam and Eve with animal skins. An animal had to be killed and sacrificed; blood was spilled to "cover" Adam. The skin also served practically as protection and shelter from the cold. Even with the failure of man and his banishment from the glory of God, God chooses to cover Adam and Eve with animal skins pointing to the sacrifice that would one day take place through Jesus, who would shed His blood to cover the multitude of sins committed by mankind.

The act of covering Adam is truly a symbol of the Son, the Supreme Lamb, who would take the place of an animal to be sacrificed. At that moment, God was sending a message to the devil: "Satan, man will remain naked, without a robe, but just as I did with Adam, one day you will see millions people wearing a new robe." Jesus gave you a new robe. Put it on and wear it!

Jesus' robe

And she gave birth to her firstborn, a son. She wrapped him in cloths and placed him in a manger, because there was no guest room available for them.
Luke 2:7

After Jesus was born in the manger, his mother Mary covered Him with cloth. The son of God was human, and naked, so man gave him clothing. When Jesus was being led away to be crucified, they put a crown of thorns on his head and mocked him: *"Are you not the King of the Jews?"* After they removed the purple robe, they gave him back a piece of cloth – just enough cloth to cover his private parts. While Jesus was on the cross, they cast lots for his clothes* (Matthew 27:35).

Jesus dies and is taken to his grave. When Mary learns that Jesus is no longer in the tomb, Peter and John run to the grave and find strips of linen and the burial cloth which had covered Jesus' face. The burial cloth covering his face was separate from the strips of linen. He had risen! However, Jesus did not resurrect wearing the cloth he was buried in. Those were clothes man had given him. The Father raised him to life and dressed him in new clothes. When she saw Jesus after His resurrection, Mary saw that the angels were all dressed in white and that Jesus was wearing a special robe – so special she could not even touch it. Do you know what robe Jesus was given when he resurrected? I believe it is the same one He wore when He spoke to the three apostles on the mountain top:

There he was transfigured before them. His face shone like the sun, and his clothes

became as white as the light.
Matthew 17:2

When Jesus was transfigured on the mountain, his clothing changed. They were not the same as before. His face was as bright as the sun. His clothes shone. In this scene, the disciples saw not only an earthly Jesus, or a bleeding Savior, but a Jesus who would be glorified and would rise from the dead. It was a vision of what would happen. Even on the mountain, God speaks about Jesus:

While he was still speaking, a bright cloud covered them, and a voice from the cloud said, "This is my Son, whom I love; with him I am well pleased. Listen to him!"
Matthew 17:5

In this wonderful vision God is saying to the disciples: "This is my Son, whom I love; with him I am well pleased." But Jesus is not naked or dressed in rags. He is wearing the robe of a Son, of a King, of the Lord of Lords, a robe for the One who is worthy of all honor, all glory, all our praise and adoration. The robe of the One who, in Revelation, is "holy, holy, holy".

What are you? A slave? A servant of the Father? We work for the Lord and serve Him out of love, but above all, we are children of God, purchased by His sacrifice on the cross. If you are a child of God, there is a new robe for you too.

You have a place in the Father's House. You are dressed as royalty. You are dressed as a child of God. You are an heir to God's Kingdom. This is the position God has given you. Even if the devil tries to dominate your mind, get up from among the pigs and go to the Father's House wearing the robe you have the right to wear. God wants to dress you in a royal robe, so do not turn it down. I pray that you will be dressed like a child of God, while you continue to learn about the House you live in.

CHAPTER 2
Jesus is in the House

A few days later, when Jesus again entered Capernaum, the people heard that he had come home. They gathered in such large numbers that there was no room left, not even outside the door, and he preached the word to them. Some men came, bringing to him a paralyzed man, carried by four of them. Since they could not get him to Jesus because of the crowd, they made an opening in the roof above Jesus by digging through it and then lowered the mat the man was lying on. When Jesus saw their faith, he said to the paralyzed man, "Son, your sins are forgiven." But some teachers of the law were sitting there, thinking to themselves, "Why does this fellow talk like that? He's blaspheming! Who can forgive sins but God alone?" Immediately Jesus knew in his spirit that this was what they were thinking in their hearts, and he said to them, "Why are you thinking these things? Which is easier: to say to this paralyzed man, 'Your sins are forgiven,' or to say, 'Get up, take your mat and walk'? But I want you to know that the Son of Man has authority on earth to forgive sins." So he said to the man, "I tell you, get up, take your mat and go home." He got up, took his mat and walked out in full view of them all. This amazed everyone and they praised God, saying, "We have never seen anything like this!"

Mark 2:1-12

I'm sure you have heard the expression: "There is no place like home". Our home, where we live, is our place of refuge and rest, where we share many life experiences. When the family lives in peace, everyone is eager to get back home.

It is home where a wife waits for her husband to arrive, where children wait for their mother, or grandchildren wait for their grandparents to visit. And when they arrive, everyone says with joy: "Your father's home!" "Mom's home!" "Grandpa's here!" Especially for children, it is always a joy to know that those who care for them and protect them are right there, at home. In Mark, chapter 2, Jesus is returning home after spending a long time away. The New Living Translation says, *"A few days later, when Jesus again entered Capernaum, the people heard that he had come home."* This is news that should spread like wildfire: *Jesus is Home!* What wonderful news! The Master is Home; the Healer is Home; the One who has the power to forgive sins is Home! In what House? The church. In what House? Your life.

You live with the Lord, Almighty! You were created in the image and likeness of God. If you have accepted Jesus into your heart, the Lord lives in your life! So your life cannot be ordinary. We, believers, are different! Wherever we go, our thoughts or attitude and behavior are different because He lives within us.

This is news that we should spread everywhere: Jesus has come Home, Jesus is in the House! It may seem obvious, but too often we go to a church meeting and leave without even remembering the main reason we were there: Jesus. He is present; He is here among us, and this conviction should

THE HOUSE | WELCOME HOME!

change our perspective completely. Church is not just a place where we gather to worship and hear a sermon. The House of God is the best place to participate in what God is doing; it is a place to be fed and hear the voice of God. In the past, non-believers thought that the church was a place for social misfits and strange or crazy people. Today, if you bring someone to church, they are surprised by what they feel and see. In the House of God, we must have His presence.

What would the house in Capernaum be like without Jesus? It would simply have been be an empty house. The house only became a Home when news spread that Jesus was there. What keeps us in the House of God is not the denomination or a famous preacher being there. It is the holy presence of Jesus! That is what makes all the difference.

So, what do we find in God's House? Let's look again at Mark, chapter 2 and see what we find. In reading the Biblical text, we see that there were four things in the house where Jesus was.

> They gathered in such large numbers that there was no room left, not even outside
> the door, and he preached the word to them.
>> Mark 2:2

The first thing we find in the House is the living Word. Jesus preached the word to them. Not just stories, but the life-giving word given by the Holy Spirit, bringing revelation, fire and nourishment. In the House where Jesus is present, the living Word is needed; words of fire, words of healing, words that give us purpose, words that give vision for the future, words that encourage us to face a new day. The Bible gives us different examples of the power in God's word:

> By faith we understand that the universe was formed at God's command, so that
> what is seen was not made out of what was visible.
>> Hebrews 11:3

> If you remain in me and my words remain in you, ask whatever you wish, and it
> will be done for you.
>> John 15:7

> The Spirit gives life; the flesh counts for nothing. The words I have spoken to you—
> they are full of the Spirit and life.
>> John 6:63

> Your word is a lamp for my feet, a light on my path.
>> Psalms 119:105

> But the word of the Lord endures forever.
>> 1 Peter 1:25

The whole universe is sustained by the word of God. Billions of stars are sustained by the word of God. The millions of planets are sustained by the power of God's word. If the Word ceased to exist, everything would disintegrate. We are sustained every day by the power of God's word. Without the Word, we would not know principles that should guide our lives and lead us in the way everlasting.

The second thing we find in the House is friendship. Friendship has led many believers out of the House and into the world. Therefore, although friendship is natural and does not seemingly have any influence or spiritual aspect, the actions of friendship are spiritual. Let's look at the passage again:

> *Some men came, bringing to him a paralyzed man, carried by four of them. Since they could not get him to Jesus because of the crowd, they made an opening in the roof above Jesus by digging through it and then lowered the mat the man was lying on.*
> Mark 2:3-4

The Scriptures say that four men carried the cripple and took him to the house where Jesus was. These four men could only have been friends! They were concerned about their paralyzed friend and took him to see Jesus because they wanted to see him healed. They knew Jesus was in the House, and so that was the place he would be healed. In the House of God, there must be friendship, but not the superficial kind. We are a part of God's family, so, the friendship between us should be the kind we offer our lives for, that is, we would pay the price to see each other's lives transformed, healed and set free. We must be able to see, help, embrace, and have compassion and mercy on others. That's how Jesus lived. The Bible says that He "was filled with compassion" for the widow in Nain, to the point of raising her son from the dead. (Luke 7:13). On another occasion, the Bible quotes Jesus himself saying: *He called His disciples to Him and said, "I have compassion for these people; they have already been with me three days and have nothing to eat"* (Matthew 15:32). He had mercy on others, and acted on their behalf! If we are to reflect Jesus, we must also allow friendship and compassion to move us toward blessing each other.

Those four men were true friends to the paralyzed man. We have no idea if they were related, if they were neighbors or just acquaintances, because the Bible does not say. However, there was a true friendship, which gave them compassion for the paralyzed man. Likewise, the church is a place of relationship, communion and friendship. We should find in the church – the House where Jesus is – the same elements found in the house of Mark 2.

There are people who make friends to benefit their own self-interest. Stay away from these kinds of people! There are friends who only want what you have, and the more you give, the more they want. When you have nothing else to give, you will be worthless to them. However, that was not the case with the friends mentioned above. Those four men were concerned with carrying their paralyzed friend on their backs and seeing him healed. They sacrificed so their friend could receive the miracle he needed! What are your friends doing to help you grow into your future? What have they contributed to your progress so far? Those men took the risk, they paid the price! Can you imagine those friends carrying the weight of that man? What kind of friendship is able to carry your weight? What friend says: "No matter the cost, I will take you to a higher place, the place you need to be. Count on me, I will help you. I will not give up until your life is transformed." What a tremendous friendship! Only God is able to create a relationship so deep that it fills us with compassion for one another.

The third thing we find in the House is prayer that leads to action.

> When Jesus saw their faith, he said to the paralyzed man, "Son, your sins are forgiven." Now some teachers of the law were sitting there, thinking to themselves, "Why does this fellow talk like that? He's blaspheming! Who can forgive sins but God alone?" Immediately Jesus knew in his spirit that this was what they were thinking in their hearts, and he said to them, "Why are you thinking these things? Which is easier: to say to this paralyzed man, 'Your sins are forgiven,' or to say, 'Get up, take your mat and walk'? But I want you to know that the Son of Man has authority on earth to forgive sins." So he said to the man, "I tell you, get up, take your mat and go home."
>
> Mark 2:2-11

Those were Jesus' words when He forgave the man's sins, and the Pharisees and Teachers of the Law were infuriated. Just imagine the scenario: remember, Jesus is in the house. The house is full of people who are there because of Jesus. They are not elbowing their way in because of a religious figure from the surrounding area, or to hear a famous scribe holding a few meetings that week. They were all there to see and hear Jesus. I imagine the atmosphere was filled with faith and prayer, honoring the tremendous presence of the One whose words caused crowds to listen in silence. It is this atmosphere of prayer that perpetuated action. Jesus had just shown the crowd that to Him, forgiving sins and healing a paralytic were the same thing. He forgave the man's sins and also healed his paralysis, proving to everyone there that the Son of Man has the power to forgive, deliver and heal.

Prayer brings action! Prayer moves heaven so things can happen. If those four men had not dared to open the roof to lower the paralytic to Jesus, perhaps that miracle would have never happened. But, moved by faith and the atmosphere in that prayer-filled place, they decided to act, and Jesus responded! There are people who only pray, but never act. If someone is unemployed and depressed, of course, they should pray; but they need to act on their faith as well. There are people who are in the same situation for years and never act on their faith.

Even if you can't see anything happening, pray with faith, hope and act according to the Word of God. Let your heart lead you to prayer rather than problems being your only reason to pray. You should seek God in prayer daily, not just when problems arise.

Another important aspect of the House is when we are certain that Jesus is present, we will always have a desire to lead others there to find Him. What do we do when we like a certain place? I am sure that when you go to a nice restaurant, where the food is good and prices are fair, you tell all your friends about it because you want them to enjoy it like you did. Isn't that true?

If we do this with restaurants, a movie or a store – which do not determine our lives or tomorrows – why not do it with the House of God? Why are there believers who do not testify to anyone? There is only one explanation: because they themselves do not believe. But anyone who loves God and sees the result in their lives will be more than happy to share. You do not have to be an evangelist; you just have to do what the word says: "Go and preach". Believers, go and speak the word; go and testify! If you find life is good in God's House, if life in the presence of God brings you joy, you will want to talk about it. You won't be able to keep silent.

Prayer and action. That's what we see in the House, both through Jesus' actions and the actions of the four men. The religious men did not get involved, but God always acts in His House. The only hindrance that can stop God from acting is our own heart. The Bible says that Jesus searched the hearts of those in the house:

> Immediately Jesus knew in his spirit that this was what they were thinking in their
> hearts, and he said to them, "Why are you thinking these things?
> Mark 2:8

Jesus knows the hearts of those in the House. If the religious Pharisees, who questioned Jesus' ability to forgive sins, had begun to repent, they too would have been forgiven. But instead, they chose to complain; to be offended and left the house upset. The cripple got up and walked home. And his four friends left give praise to God.

It is important to remember that those four men also acted. They believed that Jesus had the power to heal, so much so that they carried the paralytic to the house where Jesus was. They did not mind the difficulties or setbacks they faced. These men are a clear example of how we should act when we invite someone to the Lord's House. We need to be prepared to face the difficulties and barriers that may arise, and never give up! Many things may have happened with the paralyzed man that could have stopped him from going to Jesus' House. But his four friends did not leave him on his mat; they did not abandon him along the way. The devil always places an obstacle in our way because he knows that the Lord will act, and so he tries to stop us. Be prepared to break through any "roof" in the name of Jesus.

The fourth thing we can see in the House is unity:

THE HOUSE | WELCOME HOME!

Some men came, bringing to him a paralyzed man, carried by four of them. Since they could not get him to Jesus because of the crowd, they made an opening in the roof above Jesus by digging through it and then lowered the mat the man was lying on.
   Mark 2:3-4

They all worked together towards the same goal. The four friends worked as a team until the end. When they reached the house where Jesus was, they realized it was full and there was no way they could enter with a stretcher. There were people in every corner of the house! So, they worked together, and found a ladder and climbed onto the roof. The four of them were on the roof. There was no one below, holding the ladder for them. They started on the ground, climbed the ladder and got up onto the roof. What an extraordinary price they paid for a paralyzed man!

Maybe you're wondering who that paralyzed man was, or what does he represent. It's simple. Anyone in this world who does not have Jesus is a paralytic. They are empty. We live in a society where many "empty" people have achieved great success. They may have achieved success and acquired fame and fortune, but they are empty. One day all of it will pass, the fame and success will be left behind, and they will not have a single coin of the real fortune. Jesus said, "But store up for yourselves treasures in heaven, where moths and vermin do not destroy, and where thieves do not break in and steal" (Matthew 6:20). We can be blessed on this earth, but the most important thing we need to have in our lives is the presence of the Lord.

The four friends were there together, paying the price on their friend's behalf, because they believed in Jesus, and so they climbed onto the roof. And because they were on the roof, Jesus "… saw their faith…" (Mark 2:5). Jesus saw the practical action the four men took by getting on the roof. They received the compliment together, as they were on the roof. Only faith put into action receives recognition. Their faith did not dwindle when they saw the house full. Their practical faith took them to the rooftop! It would have done no good to have all that faith if Jesus had not been in the house. There is no use in having faith in anything but God Almighty. If we do not believe in God, then our faith is in vain.

This verse also tells us that Jesus was not moved by the condition of the paralytic. He acted because of the faith of those four men. This is Biblical. When Jesus saw their faith, he said to the paralyzed man, "Son, your sins are forgiven" (Mark 2:5). We must understand that our faith must be based upon the word. God has no commitment to man, but He is committed to His Word. And a man who lives by the word is a man of faith. He who believes will see the results.

That day, the house in Capernaum was full of faith and miracles, but there was also room for criticism and religiosity. When Jesus saw the paralytic being lowered from the roof, He saw an opportunity to confront the spirit of religion with the truth, that His Father had sent Him to forgive sins and reconcile man with God. Through this reconciliation, man would receive back everything

God had prepared for him.

For too long the Church has only taught us that by accepting Jesus, we will be saved and go to Heaven, but it has not taught that much about life here on earth. Consequently, many believers did not live a life of victory here on earth. They were oppressed, just waiting to go to Heaven. But, truth is, those who have accepted Jesus experience Heaven here on earth! Our lives begin to express Jesus right here on earth, because He lives within us. This is wonderful!

Unfortunately, we still see people with the same attitude as the Pharisees today. They did not want to learn, or to change their ways; they were not open to the truth. They were devoted to their false doctrine! To them, the Law and legalism were greater than God. Since they did not repent and receive forgiveness for their sins, they did not receive what the paralytic received.

Before addressing the paralytic, Jesus said to the Pharisees: "Which is easier? Telling the cripple: Your sins are forgiven; or to say: Stand up, take your mat and walk away?" The devil destroyed man through sin. Jesus came as a man to earth to destroy sin! "But I want you to know that the Son of Man has authority on earth to forgive sins." So he said to the man, "I tell you, get up, take your mat and go home." (Mark 2:10-11).

This is the authority the church has! Those who are planted in the House of God should not just sit there and give offerings! We are called to do much more than that. We must be rooted in the church and have a commitment to God. God reveals Himself to the world through people. You need to show the world that the Lord is in His House, and that He is in your life!

The Lord must be in us, and we need to be in His House, the church. We need to have a commitment and a covenant with the House of God, because everyone who is in the House is blessed. What was the result of Jesus being in that house? Everyone, not just the paralytic and his friends, was able to say, "We have never seen anything like this!" (Mark 2:12). Stay in the House, and prepare yourself to see things you have never seen before.

CHAPTER 3
Picking up the cloak

Ejliah took his cloak, rolled it up and struck the water with it. The water divided to the right and to the left, and the two of them walked across a dry riverbed. When they had crossed, Elijah said to Elisha, "Tell me, what can I do for you before I am taken from you?" (…) Elisha then picked up Elijah's cloak that had fallen from him and went back and stood on the bank of the Jordan. He took the cloak that had fallen from Elijah and struck the water with it. "Where now is the LORD, the God of Elijah?" he asked. When he struck the water, it divided to the right and to the left, and he crossed over.

2 Kings 2:8-1

Just imagine if someone you really admired, a person who you had seen doing incredible things, defying all logic, gave you an opportunity to ask for whatever you wished. What would you ask for? It is not uncommon to find people who, even when faced with great adversities, never stop to reflect upon what they should ask God for – they just keep asking for the same obvious things over and over: a house, food, a job. But what could you ask for that would really transform your life?

I was told a story about a family who lived in extreme poverty and could never seem to improve their circumstances. A father, mother, four children and two grandparents lived in a small, humble house. They all wore old, ragged clothes. Every day, at lunch and dinner the family gathered around their meager meal to thank God and ask Him for help: "Oh God, help us! Help us prosper and get out of our desperate situation!" The family's sole possession was a cow. Everything revolved around that cow, because it provided the milk which fed the family every day. All they did was feed the cow, milk the cow, and care for the cow. But one day, the cow died. The family was devastated because they had no hope for the future, and questioned God about their misfortune: "Oh God, is this how you answer our prayers and solve our problems?" However, a year after the cow died, the lives of the entire family changed. The small house had become a large house. The family now wore new, clean clothes and proud smiles. After the death of their cow and the distress that followed, the family had had to find another source of food. So they planted a garden on a large plot of land they owned, and in time, they began to produce more than enough for themselves and started selling the extra produce to local markets. The death of their only "safety net" had opened doors to a new way of life and made them see new possibilities! Often times we do not know how to ask, because we cannot evaluate the circumstances around us and see what is best for us. If your past is filled with difficulties, maybe you are accustomed to thinking only about day-to-day survival, and have not learned how to think boldly in regards to your perspective for tomorrow.

What would you have done if you were Elisha? Imagine the difficult moment he was experiencing and what thoughts must have gone through his mind. He was only a young farmer from the Jordan Valley when Elijah called him to serve him.

THE HOUSE | WELCOME HOME!

So Elijah went from there and found Elisha son of Shaphat. He was plowing with twelve yoke of oxen, and he himself was driving the twelfth pair. Elijah went up to him and threw his cloak around him. Elisha then left his oxen and ran after Elijah. "Let me kiss my father and mother goodbye," he said, "and then I will come with you." "Go back," Elijah replied. "What have I done to you?" So Elisha left him and went back. He took his yoke of oxen and slaughtered them. He burned the plowing equipment to cook the meat and gave it to the people, and they ate. Then he set out to follow Elijah and became his servant.
1 Kings 19:19-21

Elisha left everything to be with Elijah. He had seen him perform miracles and wonders, and had come to admire him. Elijah had been his master, walking alongside him and teaching him the ministry of a prophet, as God had commanded: The Lord said to him, "Go back the way you came, and go to the Desert of Damascus … And Elisha the son of Shaphat of Abel Meholah you shall anoint as prophet in your place" (1 Kings 19:15-16). Now Elisha was before a man who would soon be leaving. Elijah caught him unawares and asked him to do something surprising: "Tell me, what can I do for you before I am taken from you?" He had served his master until the very end, and now he had the chance for a single request. Now what? What should I ask for? I will be alone without the protection of Elijah. Should I ask for a brand new car? A house on the beach? Maybe lifelong income? If the Master stood before you today, what would you ask for? Elisha made a bold choice. It did not matter that he was letting go of other, "safer" requests. Elisha wanted to see tremendous things in his life! He had seen what Elijah had done and he would not be content living any differently.

Moments before, Elijah and Elisha had been walking side by side. Elijah took his cloak, rolled it up, struck the water in the River Jordan, and the river opened up. They left the Promised Land and crossed on dry land to the other side. Elijah insisted that Elisha leave him, he repeated three times: "Stay here; the Lord has sent me to Bethel," but Elisha's reply was always the same: "As surely as the Lord lives and as you live, I will not leave you" (2 Kings 2). Maybe some of us would have given up at Elijah's insistence, but not Elisha. He would go with Elijah until the very end.

The Bible emphasizes the importance of persevering to the end without giving up. "Be faithful, even to the point of death, and I will give you life as your victor's crown" (Revelation 2:10). "If you remain in me and I in you, you will bear much fruit" (John 15:5). Faithfulness is one of the secrets to staying in the House of God and discovering His purpose for our lives. Many of us begin the journey well, like Elisha, but are not faithful, and end up giving up! It is easier to give up in the face of opposition than to stand up and boldly move ahead, with faith in what God has promised, and will fulfill. However, only those who are steadfast will remain. Are you ready to persevere and not give up, like Elisha and so many other men of God?

Elisha received a great reward for his perseverance. He heard the man of God: What do you want me to do? What would we ask of God? I imagine you would have many things to ask of

God – you probably have a pretty long list! Let's take a look at what Elisha asked Elijah.

> *When they had crossed, Elijah said to Elisha, "Tell me, what can I do for you*
> *before I am taken from you?" "Let me inherit a double portion of your spirit,"*
> *Elisha replied.*
> 2 Kings 2:9

How bold! Elisha could have asked for many things, but he asked for something that placed great responsibility on himself. And, Elijah did not ignore Elisha, on the contrary, he recognized Elisha had made a serious request: "You have asked a difficult thing", said the prophet (2 Kings 2:10). God loves people who know how to ask for things! God loves those whose requests are in line with His will.

 Elisha asked for a double portion of Elijah's spirit. However, Elijah did have one condition: "Yet if you see me when I am taken from you, it will be yours—otherwise, it will not." (2 Kings 2:10). In other words, Elijah was telling Elisha that his request depended upon him! What you're asking for is up to you, Elisha!

When Elijah attached a condition to the request, he was teaching Elisha that the answer depended only on him. It didn't depend on Elijah, but on Elisha himself. Elijah's condition, "if you see me" didn't only mean that Elisha would have to see Elijah ascending, it had a deeper meaning as well: it meant seeing him as his father.

When the moment of Elijah's rapture came, a whirlwind appeared bringing a chariot and horses of fire, and Elisha said: "My father, my father, the chariots and horsemen of Israel!" (2 Kings 2:12). Elisha did not only see Elijah being taken, but at that moment, he understood what his master had meant when he said: "if you see me." So, he shouted "My father, my father."

Let me ask you a question: when you look at your leader, what do you see first? Power? Fire? Glory? Or do you see a father?

The first thing that Elisha saw was a father figure. His reference was very clear when he exclaimed "My father, my father." The first thing Elisha saw in Elijah was the example of a man. Elisha followed him, respected him, and knew Elijah very well. Why? Because through Elijah he was able to know God Almighty.

You cannot know God through nature: you cannot know God through the Sun or moon; you cannot know God through the sea. People may recognize God through His creation, which proves His existence, but that is not enough to really know Him. God can only be known when He reveals Himself to us, and He can only do that through His servants. Elisha was able to know God through Elijah. And, that is the reason he recognized a father figure in the prophet. By walking at his side, Elisha saw an example of a man who knew, obeyed and served God in every way, which was confirmed by the signs that followed him.

In the New Testament, we have a great example of this in the apostle Paul. He says in 1 Corinthians 11:1: "Follow my example, as I follow the example of Christ." Paul was not worried about his reputation; he would do anything to glorify the name of Christ, and the glory of God was manifested in his life. Paul had the authority to speak in this way because he walked with God; he knew God and always tried to follow Him. How can you imitate God if you cannot at least see Him in your life?

To be an imitator of Christ, first there must be a channel through which you can know who He is. God uses different channels to reveal Himself to you. He used powerful men in the past, and still is using men and women who want to manifest His glory on earth. The ways of this world have dominated people, but God is raising up a church full of grace and power, which reflects the presence of God, a church that can really change history.

To be able to change history, we need to learn to ask like Elisha did. Some people only want chariots and horses of fire. But Elisha said "My father, my father." What do you admire in your leader, and hope to receive from them? Do you just want the fire? Or perhaps you just want the power? Maybe you only want the gifts your leader has? What do you see when you look at someone who is a spiritual reference point in your life? There are people who seek the gifts, talents or even the ministry of their leaders; others want the fire, glory and power. Some people desire the success, fame and personal benefits their leader has, while others want the same authority they see in their leader.

When we are a part of the Kingdom of God, the House of God, we must learn and understand the principles that govern it. An important lesson we can learn from the example of Elijah and Elisha is that genuine power from God brings responsibility.

I'm sure you have known leaders who were famous for what they had accomplished, but unfortunately they did not persevere until the end. It is not fame or power that keeps us standing, but obedience to the principles of the Kingdom of God. And that applies to everyone who is a part of it, no matter what position we may be in. They are the principles that keep the House standing! They keep a church alive, healthy and powerful! It is not the liturgy in a service or the amount of attractions presented to its members that keep the church alive. The church is not a venue for entertainment; it is a place where God manifests His glory and His power.

> *"His intent was that now, through the church, the manifold wisdom of God should be made known to the rulers and authorities in the heavenly realms, according to his eternal purpose that he accomplished in Christ Jesus our Lord."*
> Ephesians 3:10-11

God wants to become known through the church; the church's mission is to manifest God's wisdom. The church is the spokesperson for God on earth, and you're a part of it.

What releases the double portion?

There are people in the church who only want the "chariots and horses", and place their expectations in the "chariots of fire"! Some even subconsciously hope that their leader will be "promoted" so they can be "promoted". When they see a powerful, supernatural event as described in 2 Kings, chapter 2, such people are attracted by the power. They only see their personal Interest and human glory.

Success is not a bad thing when it is based on the correct principles. But success without principles is short-lived. And this truth not only applies to the church; but to everyone because it is a principle established by God. Anything that is not built on a firm foundation will eventually fall! But, I have good news: God is building a church with a strong foundation! Winds and storms may come, but it will remain standing because it is rooted in the principles of God!

Many may wonder why Elisha asked for a double portion. Was he being greedy? In truth, it is not wrong to desire great things. The problem lies in how we ask for them: what are our motives; why do we desire it; what do we hope to accomplish?

When he asked for a double portion, Elisha was asking for an inheritance reserved for the eldest child. In Deuteronomy 21:17, Moses established a law which detailed the inheritance of the firstborn:

> *"He must acknowledge the son of his unloved wife as the firstborn by giving him a double share of all he has. That son is the first sign of his father's strength. The right of the firstborn belongs to him."*
> Deuteronomy 21:17

This verse describes the institution of the Law of the Firstborn. In other words, the eldest son was entitled, by inheritance, to a double portion. When he asked for a double portion, Elisha was not making a flippant request. He was asking as a son, because he considered Elijah his father! And that is why he requested what is written in the law of Moses. Elisha asked for his inheritance! He was in the position of a son, and as such, was entitled to a double portion from Elijah. This feeling is so strong within Elisha that he repeats the phrase twice – "my father", and the emphasis reveals what was in his heart. To qualify for the inheritance of the eldest son, you had to have a father! There is no double portion without a father.

THE HOUSE | WELCOME HOME!

The House of God

What does God mean in your life? What does House of God mean to you? How do you see your leader or pastor? Who do you submit to? Who do you obey? Unfortunately, there are people around us who proudly say: I do not submit to anyone. My pastor is Jesus Christ and I am part of an invisible church!

This is a powerful principle that God is speaking about all over the world, calling the attention of thousands to see the need to acknowledge God in someone, and that someone has to be a person you can trust, someone of whom you can say, "The Lord is with him."

You may have been disappointed with a leader or hurt by their attitude, and this has driven you away from the church. However, it is very important for you to understand that maintaining this feeling in your heart will only increase the sadness in your spirit. The devil will try to use this to distract you from what is most important, and will attempt to take you to hell with him. Remember, there is no double portion without a father.

We live in a generation where people do not honor their parents. Most young people do not honor their parents, teachers or any other authority figure. We hear stories of children who beat their parents, students who fight with their teachers to do whatever they want. Within God's House, however, the principles of God must prevail. When you apply God's principles to your life, you will see a revolution in everything around you. Even the universe will be impacted by you, and your life will not be ordinary, but powerful! You will stop being a "believer" in name only, and become a powerful instrument in the hands of God! You will not be an "echo", but the very voice of God!

This principle of authority is very serious, and must be respected. One day, Elisha was traveling to a city, and on the way, a group of young people began making fun of him.

> From there Elisha went up to Bethel. As he was walking along the road, some boys came out of the town and jeered at him. "Get out of here, baldy!" they said. "Get out of here, baldy!" He turned around, looked at them and called down a curse on them in the name of the LORD. Then two bears came out of the woods and mauled forty-two of the boys.
> 2 Kings 2:23-24

A group of forty-two young people were killed by two bears for having mocked the prophet! But why was their punishment so harsh? To learn to respect men of God. It is fundamental for us to understand the seriousness of the principle of respect for God-given authority. By failing to uphold this principle, you might not be attacked by bears, but you will certainly face serious consequences.

There are people who spend their whole lives moving from one place to another, looking for a church, looking for a place to go every Sunday. Such a person can waste their whole life away just walking around, and risk finding themselves face to face with the devil! I am not concerned with just filling the church; my main concern is when the service ends and people go home; what is going on in their day to day lives. Within the four walls of the church, it is easy to say we love God and worship Him; but when the church building empties that is when the church must be at work in the world.

When the service ends and you return home, is your life the same as those outside the church? You need to be what God wants you to be! To receive the inheritance of the eldest, you need a father. It is easy to say: "God is my father, the Lord is with me." But He will only become your Father when you begin to respect others, submit to those in authority and recognize God in their lives. God is in Heaven, but he is revealed through his instruments here on earth.

It is important that you have a devotional time alone with God to develop your relationship with Him, but nothing substitutes being in church. Nothing can replace the fellowship we have with other believers and how God manifests Himself when we are together.

I can personally say that we face opposition to get to the House of God. I know, from my own experiences, that there are many barriers against being at church. My mother was a believer, but she could never get me to go to church. I was proud to say that even though my mother was a believer, I was not! But, one day when I entered the House of God, I found that He was there waiting for me. That day he came into my life and turned everything upside down! I left that place saying, I know that my Redeemer lives!

Many believers are in church just to seek a double blessing, but they don't know if they have a father. Every religion promises blessings, but the question is what do we do after we receive the blessing? What do we do after we are healed? I have seen God heal the sick on many occasions, but the question is what do these people do after they are healed?

Some people only come to church when they have some kind of problem, whether financial, family, emotional or spiritual. But when everything begins going well again, they disappear from church. What do we do after we are freed? Healed? Employed?

Do not seek God only when you are in trouble. God is much more than a healer, He is much more than a liberator. If it were not so, Job would have just given up. His body was covered with tumors; he was alone, without any friends. His children had died and he had lost all his possessions. His fortune would be worth nearly thirty billion dollars today, and he lost it all. This is the man who said:

THE HOUSE | WELCOME HOME!

"I know that my redeemer lives, and that in the end he will stand on the earth.
And after my skin has been destroyed, yet in my flesh I will see God".
Job 19:25-26

God is raising up a church completely passionate for Him and His word, that loves being in His House, the place of His presence. I love God, and I am so glad to see so many men who love Him just as much, bringing the Presence of God into my life. It is so good to see the instruments of God ministering words that bless us. This is exactly what Elisha saw first; he saw a father in Elijah, not his power, success or glory. Elijah was the reference point Elisha had for God.

I know people who have become church experts. They know everything about liturgy, doctrine, denominations, they know all the different varieties and trends of the "gospel", but they do not know the Father nor recognize the instruments chosen by God to bless their lives!

A Question of DNA

"Now Elisha had been suffering from the illness from which he died. Jehoash
king of Israel went down to see him and wept over him. "My father! My father!"
he cried. "The chariots and horsemen of Israel!"
2 Kings 13:14

Can you see the parallel between this verse and the one in which Elijah is taken to heaven? In 2 Kings 3, the prophet Elisha becomes sick with a illness that would kill him. Elisha was dying. Who goes to visit him? The king of Israel, Jehoash, whose name means "disobedient". The Bible tells us that he cries over Elisha and says: "My father! My father! The chariots and horsemen of Israel," the very same expression used by Elisha when Elijah was ascending. However, there is a big difference between them. After all, God does not feel pain from the tears we shed if they are not true to what is in our hearts. God is interested in our brokenness and repentance much more than in our tears.

Jehoash wanted something from Elisha, but he did not have the same spirit. Jehoash did not have the same spiritual DNA as Elisha, even though he called him father. What was really behind Jehoash's tears and his desire to have Elisha as a "father" was his interest in ridding Israel of their troubles. He calls "my father, my father" out of his own self interest.

If you are a teenager, or a young person reading this book, receive this Word into your heart, and you will overcome demons you never imagined existed! They will not have any influence over your life anymore because the Word of God will be established within you. The principles of the Word will be inside you, and once more: you will be amazed at what God will do during the course of your life.

King Jehoash was a young ruler, much younger than Elisha was. And although he refers to him as father with his lips, in his heart he did not have the spirit of Elisha, the essence of Elisha. In other words, he did not know nor imitate the attitudes and behavior of Elisha. He did not know how Elisha thought, since he never followed him nor was his disciple. The only thing that Jehoash knew was that Elisha was a prophet, and when he opened his mouth the words spoken really happened! Jehoash went to see the prophet only to rid himself from his afflictions. Israel was being defeated in war after war. Their enemies were rising up and oppressing the nation. As king of Israel, Jehoash had to take a stand and do something about the situation. So he remembered the prophet, but he needed to act quickly, because Elisha was seriously ill.

> "Now Elisha had been suffering from the illness from which he died. Jehoash king of Israel went down to see him and wept over him. "My father! My father!" he cried. "The chariots and horsemen of Israel!" Elisha said, "Get a bow and some arrows," and he did so. "Take the bow in your hands," he said to the king of Israel. When he had taken it, Elisha put his hands on the king's hands. "Open the east window," he said, and he opened it. "Shoot!" Elisha said, and he shot. "The LORD's arrow of victory, the arrow of victory over Aram!" Elisha declared. "You will completely destroy the Arameans at Aphek."
> 2 Kings 13:14-17

Let's imagine this scene. Jehoash approaches Elisha and with a sad countenance said these words: "My father, my father"! Elisha is not moved by what he hears, and gives specific instructions: Get the bow, open the window, point to the east and shoot over the ground. That was the word burning in Elisha's heart. He could see total victory for Israel. The spirit of Elisha was filled with faith, but Jehoash did not have the same feeling inside. He was obedient, but he did not have the same faith that Elisha had. His DNA was different; his vision was different; he could not see within his spirit the great victory God had for His people. He did not believe that the God of Israel could perform such an extraordinary deliverance, and that's why he only struck the ground three times! He did not have the warrior spirit that was in Elisha.

On the other hand, when Elisha asked Elijah for a double portion of his spirit, he was asking for the same faith! He wanted the same faithfulness and obedience, but double. The life of Elijah was a reference for Elisha. He did not only want the miracles or wonders which God performed through Elijah, he wanted to be like him, and to have twice the intimacy that Elijah had with God. He wanted to become a reference himself.

THE HOUSE | WELCOME HOME!

A reference point

A leader should be a reference. People need a reference, or else they will follow false references. The world is crying out for leaders. The current condition of our society is proof that the leaders humanity has produced over the years did not have the necessary qualities and characteristics to fulfill their role. We live in a real crisis as far as effective leadership is concerned. The world is full of weak leaders, who cannot be considered examples to be followed.

Elijah was an example for Elisha, and this could have been an example for Jehoash, but he did not have the same spirit that Elisha did! Unlike the example of Elijah and Elisha, Jehoash did not want to be like Elisha. He did not have the same DNA, although Elisha was an example of a leader to be followed. Jehoash only wanted an instant blessing, the deliverance of Israel – a blessing from Elisha.

It's easy to receive step by step instructions telling us exactly what to do! We have learned that when we receive the Word, we have to put it into practice so it can be fulfilled. This means we must live it out in our daily lives! Elisha was telling Jehoash: *Son, you want the word of a prophet? Shoot the arrow through the window, the arrow of God's victory, the arrow of victory over the Arameans!* The prophet was not only offering a solution, but he was teaching Jehoash what path he should take. But since he did not have the same spirit as the prophet, he did not understand the entire message. Jehoash lost the opportunity to conquer the Arameans forever! Elisha had to put his hand on Jehoash's because he was trembling with insecurity. Jehoash was not able to discern the prophetic moment and the opportunity he was being offered.

The act of striking the arrows on the ground was prophetic. The arrows represented Israel, the House of God. Elisha was trying to show Jehoash that complete victory was his for the taking but Jehoash did not understand. He only obeyed, but he was not in tune with what the heart of the prophet was telling him. When he struck the ground only three times, the prophet became angry. Elisha wanted Jehoash to act like a true warrior, and strike the arrows many times. I can imagine how passively Jehoash struck the ground. He just followed the instructions the prophet had given him, but he did not do it with faith.

And this was so because Jehoash did not see Elisha as a father, but only as a magician. Elisha was not a reference to God for him. Jehoash did not walk with Elisha, and even though he called him father, he didn't truly see him that way. Like many believers in God's House today, Jehoash only sought the benefits; he was only interested in winning the war. He missed the opportunity to walk with God through the life of Elisha. He just wanted to be a successful king and have his name go down in history as the great king who defeated the Arameans!

If you pray to God for a job, He will give you legs so you can run after one; if you ask for love, He will place troubled people in your path so that you can learn to love. Sometimes we ask for blessings and God allows problems to pop up so we can obtain the blessing we prayed for.

God is more pleased to see us walk in faith and obey His Word, than in doing "magic tricks" that change everything in the blink of an eye. Though, it is easier for us to walk in faith and obey when we have a father, a "reference" to God in our lives.

But, too many times we want the supernatural to intervene in natural situations, and we want explanations for everything. Jehoash did not say it aloud, but I am sure inside he had many "whys" regarding the word he had received from Elisha. Since he did not understand the supernatural aspect of the word he received, he struck the ground only three times, and that was exactly how many times Israel defeated the Arameans.

Elisha wanted to see if Jehoash had really understood the prophetic message. Elisha wanted to see Jehoash strong, bold and full of faith. He wanted to see Jehoash striking the ground as if he could see the enemy falling one by one! He didn't want to see a man full of fear and doubt, but a man who understood the timing and opportunity of God; not a passive, weak man, but a man with a brave, conquering spirit, a spirit of a warrior! Instead, the man who stood before him was shy and had no backbone.

There are times when we just cannot use logic. Instead, we must behave like a crazy person to achieve what God has for us. Many times we will never receive an explanation, but we must have faith in what God has said. Elisha wanted Jehoash to act upon his words with faith, but the king did not understand and lost his opportunity. Elisha wanted to see Jehoash act with strength, but it never happened. If Jehoash could have understood that the power and strength of God was in the man of God who was dying and believed it, Israel would have defeated their enemies and none of them would have been left to tell the story!

Elisha was dying because his time had come, but the Spirit of God Almighty was still within him. Although he was young and healthy, Jehoash harbored the spirit of death inside him, and he missed the opportunity to receive the life that was inside the prophet. For Elisha, however, not even death could hold back the power of God.

> "Once while some Israelites were burying a man, suddenly they saw a band of raiders; so they threw the man's body into Elisha's tomb. When the body touched Elisha's bones, the man came to life and stood up on his feet."
> 2 Kings 13:21

If God allowed Elisha's bones to revive a dead man, imagine what He could have done with Jehoash! God wants to accomplish extraordinary things through all of us. We have to give credit to the men of God who have been raised up by the Lord at this time to release prophetic words over our lives. We need to learn to value what God speaks through the prophetic ministry of the Church. We must believe in the prophets that God has raised up in this time to give direction to His people!

The prophet gave an order: "Shoot." When the prophet speaks, do not try to understand, just obey. Jehoash just repeated the phrase "My father! My father! The chariots and horsemen of Israel." There's no use in repeating what has worked in the lives of others; you must have the same spirit inside of you that they had!

Many problems could be avoided if we listened to the experienced people God has placed around us. I remember when my daughters were in preschool and they spent part of the day in school. They did not mind so much because my wife, Juçara, worked at the same school at the time, but that is not common for most children. They have to be separated from their mother for part of the day. Have you ever noticed the tantrums and whining at the door of the school the first few days of class? I'm not sure who suffers the most, the mothers or the children, but even so, parents cannot keep their kids out of school. They understand that school is important; it is a place where their children will learn to read, write and interact with other children. After finishing elementary school and high school, people head for college because they recognize the fact that professors are experienced, and can pass on valuable knowledge and skills to them. After finishing college, many become doctors, lawyers, and journalists, because at some prior point they were influenced by people who became examples or references for them.

It's the same in the House of God. You have to respect, submit yourself and honor the men of God who are in authority over you. Sometimes we find more fear of God in the world than in the House of God. I know business owners who do not hire believers to work for them because during work hours, they are praying or reading the Bible instead of working! They arrive to work late and use the excuse of being at an all-night prayer meeting!

The House of God is a place of respect and order. Even people who are not part of the church are changing the way they see us. The House of God is a place where men and women are seen as references or examples, instruments of God for blessing those around them!

If you do not have a reference in your life, you are one step away from being destroyed. Jehoash did not want what the prophet had; he wanted the prophet's blessing. The only reason he even called him "My father, my father" was out of convenience. He was looking for something easy, but the prophet taught him that he could be victorious.

Sometimes when we hear a prophetic word, it is not only to change a specific situation, but also to change our perspective of it! That was what the prophet wanted Jehoash to understand: he could definitely defeat the Arameans. However, Jehoash only struck the ground three times. His vision was limited and he missed a unique opportunity to become a great warrior.

There are some people who only get close to the prophet to receive a blessing, instead of walking alongside them and learning from them! For me, one of the most rewarding things is when a young man or teenager comes up to me and tells me that I am a reference or example for their life.

If you have an example, you begin to experience the same things they do. And that includes things in the natural too. Sometimes a brother will call me to come bless their recently acquired company, and if I wait too long, when I get there I might find that the same brother has already bought an even bigger company! There are times when we will be called to minister at a funeral, but when we get there, it will have been canceled because the dead have been brought back to life! Now is the time for the church to show God's power.

The blessing of following a leader

People want to receive blessings, but we do not always want to pay the price to have the Lord's blessing. To have the Lord's blessing, you must have the Spirit of the Lord who blesses. Blessings serve only to attract us to the One who blesses. The Gospel is much more than receiving gifts, which in no way diminishes the miracles God has done in our lives. It is great to see people being healed and receiving financial miracles, but according to the principles of the Gospel, these are just signs that God lives within us.

Although they used the same expression, Elisha and Jehoash did not receive the same things. The first received Elijah's cloak, while the latter received nothing. The examples of these two men show us that within the Kingdom of God, things only work when they are under His principles. If you are living your life according to the principles of the word of God, the blessings of God will overtake you. Elisha was a follower, but Jehoash followed only his own self-interest. There is no shame in being a follower, because that is what a disciple does: they follow and imitate the masters.

We must follow God's principles and the examples He places in our lives, because He is preparing a new generation of men and women who understand God's purpose for their lives and will love and serve Him, not with their own strength or to look out for their own interests, but full of the anointing and presence of God. This new generation will change the history of this nation and the other nations of the world!

The main example we should all follow is Jesus. He said it Himself: *"Come, follow me," Jesus said, "and I will make you fishers of men."* (Matthew 4:19) In other words, Jesus was saying: *Follow my example*! However, we must be careful not to take this too literally. The examples we see of Jesus in the Word of God are to be our main references, but we cannot forget that God provides us with people – pastors, leaders, and teachers – as examples to be followed here on earth.

THE HOUSE | WELCOME HOME!

After all, it would be too easy to say we follow only Jesus and obey only Him, and not submit ourselves to human authorities. Do not be fooled. That is a big mistake!

When He said "Come, follow me," Jesus was here on earth, He was flesh and blood. Jesus was divine, but He was also human. He is proof that we should follow the people who lead us to God, who lead us to the Father, who teach and guide us from what they receive from God. Jesus is the greatest example we will ever have, but He also provides leaders for us to follow.

It does not matter if you went to seminary or know the entire Bible by heart. You need to obey God's principles, even if you do not understand them. If you are not submitted to them, you will not reach the spiritual realm of the Kingdom. Because when you submit, you also honor, learn and obey, and this is part of the culture in the Kingdom of God.

The quality of tomorrow's leader is in the character of today's follower! Our character, how we live our lives and show respect makes a difference. Whoever speaks badly of their leader is bringing curses upon their life, and their children will be first to suffer!

The Bible tells us that Elijah dropped his cloak. What does that mean? *"Elisha then picked up Elijah's cloak that had fallen from him and went back and stood on the bank of the Jordan."* Elijah ascended, but he left his cloak for Elisha.

You will always have something in your life to remind you of your leader! You will always have something to remind you of your spiritual father. That is why Elijah left his cloak behind.

After picking up the cloak, Elisha took the cloak that had fallen from Elijah and struck the water with it and said, "Where now is the Lord, the God of Elijah?".

Note that he does not say "Where is the God of heaven?" or "Where is God, the creator of the universe?" He says: "Where now is the Lord, *the God of Elijah*?".

Then the waters divided and Elisha walked across the riverbed. He spoke to the God of the man who was an example in his life; he referred to the God of his leader, who at that moment began to be a part of his life too. That cloak was not a holy mantle for Elisha, but a reminder of who Elijah was to him. Elisha took the cloak as a symbol of prophetic anointing.

The Bible mentions twice that Elisha used the cloak that Elijah dropped as a sign of honoring Elijah. It is as if Elisha was saying: "Elijah left this cloak behind for me! Elijah left a sign and certainly his God will manifest Himself in my life too." When you are a follower, you are entitled to receive the mantle your leader is wearing.

Did King Jehoash take Elisha's cloak? No! But Elisha took the one belonging to Elijah! You will always have something to remind you of whoever was an inspiration in your life. But remember that when he picked up the cloak, Elisha did not worship it. He understood perfectly that the power was not in the cloak, but in the God of Elijah! And it was this God that Elisha called to divide the River Jordan. The cloak represented the anointing; therefore when the cloak fell and Elisha picked it up, there was a transfer of the prophetic anointing from Elijah to Elisha, but with one big difference: Elisha received a double portion of anointing!

By receiving the cloak, Elisha intended to continue everything that God had begun in the life of Elijah – but Elisha would receive a double portion! So there was transference of a life surrendered to God, a life devoted to loving and serving the Lord – but Elisha had a mission to do twice as much as Elijah did! Would you be that bold?

If you have the same DNA, you have the same cloak; if you have the same DNA, you have the same anointing. The cloak that Elisha now possessed would also open paths for him. The same path God had opened for Elijah would now be opened for Elisha.

When Elisha crossed the River Jordan, his feet did not get wet. He walked along a miraculous path! Anything can happen when you begin to believe. Elisha could have saved the cloak as a keepsake and not done anything. He could have shed tears because he missed Elijah, but he did not. He knew that the God who had used Elijah's life could use his too, because someone who was an example in his life had taught him this. There were fifty prophets on the other side of the river, in Jericho, who saw what happened to the water, and they said: "The spirit of Elijah is resting on Elisha." And they came to meet him and bowed to the ground before him (2 Kings 2:15). Elisha believed, and the glory of God fell upon him and was recognized by those around him.

You do not have to understand everything, because not everything that God does has an explanation. But you must have faith in everything that He has said about your life. Elisha was bold when he asked and was granted his request, and he did twice as much as Elijah, for the glory of God Almighty! God used him as a powerful instrument during his life. And the same thing can happen with you!

If you believe and obey, God will use you. Follow the Godly examples in your life and be prepared to pick up the mantle when it falls to the ground. Stay in the House of God and you will receive the benefits of following the principles of God's Kingdom.

CHAPTER 4
For the common good

MARCO A. PEIXOTO

All the believers were one in heart and mind. No one claimed that any of their possessions was their own, but they shared everything they had. With great power the apostles continued to testify to the resurrection of the Lord Jesus. And God's grace was so powerfully at work in them all that there were no needy persons among them. For from time to time those who owned land or houses sold them, brought the money from the sales and put it at the apostles' feet ... The apostles performed many signs and wonders among the people. And all the believers used to meet together in Solomon's Colonnade. No one else dared join them, even though they were highly regarded by the people. Nevertheless, more and more men and women believed in the Lord and were added to their number. As a result, people brought the sick into the streets and laid them on beds and mats so that at least Peter's shadow might fall on some of them as he passed by. Crowds gathered also from the towns around Jerusalem, bringing their sick and those tormented by impure spirits, and all of them were healed.
        Acts 4:32-35; 5:12-16

It is time for a new season. I say this because just as we can see the signs of each passing season during the year, such as changes in temperature, changes in leaves and flowers, the wind direction and the position of the sun, the same thing happens in the spiritual realm. The arrival of a new season is announced with signs, as Jesus Himself taught: "When evening comes, you say, 'It will be fair weather, for the sky is red,' and in the morning, 'Today it will be stormy, for the sky is red and overcast.' You know how to interpret the appearance of the sky, but you cannot interpret the signs of the times?" (Matthew 16:2-3) In other words, Jesus is saying to just look for the signs of change to realize it is coming.

A few generations ago, believers were considered by society to be old-fashioned, alienated, ignorant and dull and, unfortunately, many times it was true. However, in recent years there has been a real change in the perception the world has of the church. Although there have been some negative aspects to go along with all the positive ones, it is undeniable that this change points to the strength of the church and its remarkable presence on earth. This is one of the signs of change we expect.

On the other hand, regardless of its apparent "strength", we must remember that as long as the church does not convey the purpose for which it was established – to manifest security, power, truth, trust, faithfulness, obedience and authority – it will never be recognized for its true value. When the church seeks to fulfill its true mission, even the wicked are impacted, because that is what the world wants to see in us: For the creation waits in eager expectation for the children of God to be revealed (Romans 8:19).

It is interesting that believers today are in the news, even in areas like politics – and the major television networks are required to report it. In recent Brazilian history, we have witnessed the influence and decisive impact of the church due to the growing number of voters who are believers. After supporting a presidential candidate who had little political influence but still finished in third place, the entire country saw the two remaining candidates fight to gain the support of "believers" in every way possible. They recognized that believers can influence the outcome of any election. We are seeing these changes happen every day. Only a few years ago, Christian events were ignored by the media, but today they are part of the news the same as regular events.

People are beginning to see the strength of the church, which was not recognized a few years ago. The evangelical church is rising, and starting to become an active part of society. However, being part of society and being recognized for our voting influence is all very good, but it is not enough! We need to be recognized by society for what we are, for our powerful testimonies, for the example of our lives as God's children.

We can learn valuable lessons about the time we are living in from the first church, as told in the book of Acts. Here, we read about the development of the church since the very beginning, when the followers of Christ first began to be called "Christians" (See Acts 11:26). After the death and resurrection of Jesus, the Holy Spirit was sent to us. About one hundred and twenty people were gathered in Jerusalem, according to Jesus' instructions, when they were all filled with the Holy Spirit. Peter began to preach boldly from that moment on. That was the beginning of the early church.

That church in the book of Acts is the example for us because it is the original church of Jesus Christ. At that time, the church was in its fullness. It had power, was growing and becoming structured. The church of Jesus was being established on earth.

Many other verses in the book of Acts describe the routine of the church back in those days. Acts 4:32 provides a wonderful description of the church: "All the believers were one in heart and mind. No one claimed that any of their possessions was their own, but they shared everything they had." This verse always reminds me of the beginning of our church, the Comunidade Internacional da Zona Sul. When we first started out, we also experienced that same sense of unity and sharing; we wanted to live as the church did in Acts! In Acts, everything belonged to everyone, they shared everything. This was the principle that governed the early church. Why? The early church was the beginning of it all. There was a lot of persecution, so they chose to always be together, in order to protect and provide for one another and further the cause of the word and their testimony. Although it is nearly impossible for the church today to work the same way, practically speaking, it is possible to live based upon the same principles.

The principles of the church in Acts are the same principles of God's word. And the principles of the Lord are unchangeable. They must be obeyed every day because, "I the Lord do not change" (Malachi 3:6). The Lord does not change, nor do His principles. The same principles that governed the church in Acts should guide the Lord's church today.

We should not disregard the teachings of God just because it is not possible to live exactly as the early church where everyone lived together and shared everything! If we cannot live the same lifestyle, then we should still live according to the principles of God's word. And these principles should govern the life of every believer.

A broken agreement

In the church of Acts, there was one thing they all agreed on: the good testimony of the brethren. There was a brother named Barnabas who sold his property, and took all the profit and laid it at the apostles' feet for the purpose of helping the poor. Apparently, this was a common practice among them: There were no needy persons among them. For from time to time those who owned land or houses sold them, brought the money from the sales" (Acts 4:34). We can not say for sure if it was part of their doctrine, but it certainly was an agreement they all put into practice.

There was a couple in the church named Ananias and Sapphira. The name Ananias means God is gracious. Ananias discovered that not only is God full of grace, but he is also holy! Unfortunately for him, he found this out too late. The couple had decided to sell some property and lay the money at the feet of the apostles, as their brother Barnabas had done. However, after the sale, Ananias and Sapphira changed their minds. They sold the property, but kept part of the money for themselves.

> Now a man named Ananias, together with his wife Sapphira, also sold a piece of property. With his wife's full knowledge he kept back part of the money for himself, but brought the rest and put it at the apostles' feet.
> Acts 5:1-2

Verse 2 states that he acted "with his wife's full knowledge." He was no longer acting according to what the Holy Spirit had spoken through the leaders of the church, thus breaking the agreement established among the brethren.

God had given them direction as to how they should live. They had made an agreement to place everything at the feet of the apostles. Ananias, however, broke this agreement with the leaders and with God, and his wife consented. By doing so, they broke the spirit of the church by doing something contrary to how the community was living, contrary to what they had seen their brother doing. Ananias and his wife did something that went against what everyone else was doing. Alone, in their own home, they decided to do something different from what they had agreed upon with the church.

THE HOUSE | WELCOME HOME!

This is where the mystery of what later happened to the couple begins to unfold. They did not lie about the price, but about their intention. Barnabas placed all the money at apostles' feet. That was the spirit of the church, a principle and an agreement they had made. But Ananias made another agreement with his wife, and brought only a portion of the money.

It is important to understand that Ananias had the right to sell his property or not, just as he had the right to give or not. They could have sold the property and kept all the money; I'm sure they would not have died over doing that. The issue was not the money, but their intentions. Ananias could have sold the property and kept all the money, and even prayed, thanking God for having blessed the sale! He could have enjoyed all the money with his wife, since it belonged to them. But that wasn't the problem.

The mistake Ananias made was to take the money and lay it at the apostles feet. He and his wife thought they could deceive the apostles. Once again, imagine this scene with me. Imagine Ananias coming to the place the apostles were gathered, and with the appearance of benevolence, laying the money at their feet. In other words, Ananias made the mistake of trying to pose as something he was not! He was a hypocrite! The sin Ananias committed was HY-PO-CRI-SY! Being a hypocrite is having the following attitude: I hear you but I do not listen. I am part of the community, but I do not follow its principles. I do whatever I please!

What did people think when they saw Ananias placing his money at the apostles' feet? What a good man! He sold his land and donated all the profits from the sale. What a man full of the Holy Spirit! That brother's heart is full of love! What a faithful man he is! He could have sold the property and done whatever he wanted with the money; after all, he owned the property! But when he placed only part of the profit at the apostles' feet, he was mocking the church.

Identifying a hypocrite

One day, a person who had backslidden was touched by the Holy Spirit and came to me and said: "Pastor, today I returned home. God embraced me; and I wept. God is here in this place, pastor. I was president of the youth group and even a deacon in my church, but I lost my way. I was disgusted with believers! I wanted nothing to do with God. I was hurt and bitter because even leaders in my own family did not practice what they preached! That left me confused and I became disgusted with the Gospel!"

There is hypocrisy in the practitioners of all religions. Religion and hypocrisy go hand in hand, together all the time. I have abhorrence to the spirit of religion and hypocrisy. Jesus also hated hypocrisy. He said these very words to the scribes and Pharisees: "Woe to you, teachers of the law and Pharisees, you hypocrites! You are like whitewashed tombs, which look beautiful on the outside but on the inside are full of the bones of the dead and everything unclean" (Matthew 23:27). People who are hypocrites are like whitewashed tombs: they look good from the outside but are rotten on the inside.

That is exactly what happened to Ananias. He stood before the people pretending to have a praise-worthy attitude, pretending to be "super-spiritual"! Although he was a part of the early church and was taught the principles of the Gospel by the apostles themselves, Ananias had not understood that the church is much more than sitting in a chair and listening; it is more than just completing scheduled rituals. The church is the living body of Christ, where we learn and grow together.

We may shepherd certain people all the time, but they may never let themselves become sheep. On the other hand, for others it simply takes a single word and they follow the word and see signs and wonders in their lives. Why does this happen? It's the heart that makes it so. When we are being guided by the Spirit of God, and are involved in a local church, we experience the release of tremendous power! Our lives grow as we become deeply rooted in the church. And even if you do not have the strength to grow on your own, your brothers and sisters will pull you up, allowing you to grow as well. The faith of the others will help you grow.

Unfortunately, that is not what happened to Ananias. He was a part of the group, but he acted according to his own will. Even more interesting is how Sapphira is reminiscent of Eve. In Acts 5:2, it says that Ananias made an agreement with his wife. And that is exactly what happened in the Garden of Eden. Adam took Eve's advice. In verse 3, Peter says to Ananias: "...Satan has so filled your heart." This reinforces that the very thing that happened in Eden happened in Acts. Satan had filled Eve's heart, and then Eve in turn filled Adam's. And we all know what happened next.

Both of these moments in history are identical. The principles are the same: Ananias only gave a portion of the money he had earned from the sale of his property. He did not flow in unity with the church. Although he was amongst the believers, he was not in tune with what God was speaking. The church was just beginning and everything was done in one accord, that is, everyone was in agreement! Life within the church depended on this principle, because that was the divine direction for that moment. Ananias was a hypocrite to his brothers – one who is with us, but is not willing to pay the same price.

God hates hypocrisy. There are other references to hypocrisy in the Bible that prove this statement: "These people honor me with their lips, but their hearts are far from me" (Matthew 15:8). Ananias tried to fake that he wasn't a man who loved money, but in his heart, it was the exact opposite. If he had kept all the money, Ananias would not have been a hypocrite. At the most, he would have been called greedy, but he would not have died.

THE HOUSE | WELCOME HOME!

Often times it is better to be honest and frank with God, or even to be "angry" with Him, than to know God but doubt in your heart, ultimately preventing you from living what you say. Such a person is "lukewarm", as described in Revelation 3:16, where God says: "Because you are lukewarm—neither hot nor cold—I am about to spit you out of my mouth." People who are lukewarm think: I am one of them, but I do not agree with them. I am with them, but I am not a part of them. On Sunday when I am at church, I raise my hands, I sing and cry but when I leave church, my actions reflect a person who loves God only inside the church; but outside of it…

Someone who truly is a part of the church, does not only practice what they hear on Sundays, but every day of their life. God enriches us and feeds us with His Word. But cursed is the man who just holds his Bible, but does not feed on the Word, because he will never hear God.

Why did Ananias die?

I want to make it very clear that Ananias did not have to offer his money. He did not have to lay it at the feet of the apostles, but since he did, he lied, because he did not give them all the money as had been agreed. And the wages of sin is death.

Let me explain why Ananias had to die. When we look at Biblical history, we see that every time God began a new period, He judged those who sinned more harshly. He revealed His principles to guide them and explained to the people what they had to do. In every moment or situation where God begins something new, the moment was treated with great seriousness and severity

Take a look, for example, at when the tabernacle was built in the Old Testament. Nadab and Abihu presented unauthorized fire to the Lord. This story is in the book of Leviticus:

> *"Aaron's sons Nadab and Abihu took their censers, put fire in them and added incense; and they offered unauthorized fire before the Lord, contrary to his command. So fire came out from the presence of the Lord and consumed them, and they died before the Lord. Moses then said to Aaron, "This is what the Lord spoke of when he said: '"Among those who approach me I will be proved holy; in the sight of all the people I will be honored.'"*
> Leviticus 10:1-3

It was a new period and God was simply building the tabernacle! The tabernacle represented the church, but it also represented man – body, soul and spirit – and pointed to God. The tabernacle was not just a place of worship; it was a place to feel the fear of the Lord.

In the tabernacle only one priest could enter the Holy of Holies each year to offer a sacrifice for the sins of the people. The priest had a rope tied around his waist and there were bells sewn to the hem of his robe. When he entered the Holy of Holies, he was to walk from side to side to keep the bells ringing. If the men outside could no longer hear them ringing, their instructions were to pull the priest out because he probably had been killed. Such was the holiness required of the priest in order to stand before the Lord and ask for the people's forgiveness. If anything went wrong, he would be killed.

The tabernacle was a very holy place, and everything was well organized according to a strict standard. God is not up in heaven just waiting for a chance to kill people. He does not impose principles on us that we cannot obey. God takes no pleasure when men die; on the contrary, he wants us all to have abundant life.

Another example occurred in the first city conquered by God's people, Jericho. As written in Joshua 6:1-27, God fulfilled his promise to His people that they would take possession of the land, but He also gave clear instructions:

> "The city and all that is in it are to be devoted to the Lord. Only Rahab the prostitute and all who are with her in her house shall be spared, because she hid the spies we sent. But keep away from the devoted things, so that you will not bring about your own destruction by taking any of them. Otherwise you will make the camp of Israel liable to destruction and bring trouble on it."
> Joshua 6:17-18

God's instructions were clear: they were to kill everyone except for Rahab, and were not to take any spoils from the city. Joshua sent this order out to all the people, but there was one who did not obey. Achan tried to play smart and disobeyed the order and took cursed things. Because of his actions, many Israeli men died in battle. Achan was stoned to death and his body burned. Whenever there is a new principle, or God is beginning something new, He establishes rules and brings righteous judgment on all those who disobey Him. It's as if God is sending a message: Do not play with My word!

In Acts, there was a new period. God was beginning the story of the church – a church which had been cleansed and redeemed through the blood of His Son, Jesus Christ.

None of us were there, but we can imagine that certain things had to be done. God wanted to raise up a holy church, but since there were some strange habits already in place, He had to remove them right from the start. So, when hypocrisy shows itself through Ananias, God does not spare him – and the result was death. Ananias and Sapphira were part of a new time in God, with a wonderful and extraordinary purpose! And, in that moment, God wanted first and foremost obedience, readiness and faithfulness to Him.

What we learn from this tragedy is that all our blessings are the result of our obedience to God. The word says: "Submit yourselves, then, to God. Resist the devil, and he will flee from you" (James 4:7). To the extent that we obey God and submit ourselves to Him, evil will flee, including the evil within us!

Obedience always brings life, and disobedience always brings death. Ananias disobeyed and suffered the consequences of his actions. And who did he disobey? The apostles! The apostles, the leaders, are the mouth of God. They are not actors or people without jobs! They are men of God, separated by God. Some people may even have doctorates in theology. Biblical education is very good, but it is not everything. The important thing is to be called by God. Men of God are called to lead and teach people, therefore, we must obey them.

The apostles had given the church a direction to follow, and when someone disobeyed, God Himself intervened. God does not want to kill anyone, nor will He do it today, but we know that whoever is hypocritical, a liar, disobedient, or does not live according to the word of God, is already spiritually dead. We have also learned that hypocrisy is the path to spiritual death and to disobeying our leaders.

Who had given the Word to be obeyed? The church leaders. The church is a place of holy fear, respect, obedience and faithfulness. We need to understand that God speaks through the mouths of man as well, and we should respect the guidance we receive in His House.

Some valuable lessons

After Ananias had died, Sapphira, his wife, arrived, looking for her husband. I can just imagine Sapphira's triumphal entrance: all pretenses, feeling like the 'woman of the year', thinking everyone was looking at her because they had given all their money to be distributed. But people were actually staring at her with fear in their eyes, because they had just seen what had happened to her husband. She must have thought that the shocked looks were because of the act of kindness she and her husband had done.

Peter called for her and asked how much the property had sold for to see if she was scheming with her husband. Sapphira repeated the same lie and Peter pronounced her death sentence – same as her husband!

It is interesting to note that neither Ananias nor Sapphira had time to use the money they had hidden. Sapphira arrived three hours later and did not know what had happened. That's what Satan does. He always leaves hypocrites in the dark. Sapphira's husband had died and she only found out three hours later! That is what the devil does with his servants: he fools them! Those that serve the devil are always behind with whatever is happening, especially when it comes to the House of God! Ananias and Sapphira died because they lied to the Holy Spirit. The Bible says in 1 Timothy 3:15: "The church of the living God, the pillar and foundation of the truth." The truth must always prevail in the church. What can we learn today from the early church?

Firstly, Peter had a spiritual discernment in the situation. We must pray for God to raise up leaders in this country with spiritual discernment. The church needs leadership that has spiritual insight. When Peter saw Ananias coming, he did not judge, because he already had discerned the situation. We need leaders who can identify what is the devil, what is the flesh, and what is from the Spirit of God.

Secondly, in Acts 5:11, it reads: "Great fear seized the whole church and all who heard about these events." So the next lesson is fear. That was what God wanted! Extraordinary respect for God came upon everyone who heard what had happened.

And thirdly, we can learn from this story in Acts 5:6: "Then some young men came forward, wrapped up his body, and carried him out and buried him." The Bible says in 1 John that young people are strong, and have overcome the evil one. In other words, they have the Word of God to overcome the devil. When Peter referred to the young men, he was calling attention to the fact that young people can be powerful in the hands of God. "Some young men came forward", in other words, when sin fell, the youth arose. And where did this happen? In the church!

There were young men in the New Testament church, and they rose up in the midst of tragedy, after Ananias fell dead. Applying this to today's church, when sin is destroyed the youth rise up! Our young people will only stand when sin is dead in the ground! Young people want to be free; they rise to the challenge. When teenagers or young people realize that the church has a future, they dive in "head first" – they want to go out into the streets, they want to do somersaults, they want to do whatever it takes to make it happen! That's how young people really are! But when there is sin, not even youth show enthusiasm. They drift away, and today many backslide because of their parents. They see the hypocrisy in their parents' lives: they act one way in church, but when they get home, they are completely different people.

The Bible tells us that young men covered Ananias' body, in other words, they covered up the sin so it would not be exposed. That's exactly what young people, the youth in God's House, should be doing. When you find someone who is dying in sin, cover them up! Do not let it spread, do not let it be seen and talked about. Do not let it become the latest news! Do not let it spread, cover it up!

We have learned that in God's House, anything related to sin cannot remain exposed. It must be covered and healed; but never left exposed! And who was responsible for this? The young men are responsible. Unfortunately, some people do not believe in young people and consider them irresponsible. But we must value young people who are filled with the Holy Spirit! Let's value this new generation, full of potential that is rising up, because they are not in church just to pass time, or to be entertained. The young men, actually, did even more: they "wrapped up his body, and carried him out and buried him." The young men removed the sin – that's what Ananias represented. They carried the body of sin out of the church. This verse teaches us that a bad testimony must be buried, and not spoken of. We must forget their actions and not talk about their mistake. If God Himself forgets and erases our sins, then who are we to bring them to life? Sin must be buried.

I hope that, through this study we have done, you can really understand why Ananias and Sapphira died. It was the beginning of a new time, and God had to be severe with sin and destroy it at the roots. God's goal was removing hypocrisy and lying from the church, uprooting those who were, deep in their hearts, not what they appeared to be! God wanted to show His people the mistake the couple had made in order to bring the fear of God into the church.

It is not God's will or purpose to go out and kill every sinner. If so, none of us would be alive now. We are nothing, but when we look to the word, we need to allow it to create fear in our hearts and live everyday according to His word, and what God says and what He wants!

Those young men buried everything that was not in accordance with the word. All hypocrisy, all disobedience, everything that is contrary to the word of God must be outside the church. The doors to our church will always be open to all kinds of people, with any kind of problem (natural, physical or spiritual), but the church is a place of transformation and recovery. Such people must be transformed from faith to faith, and glory to glory, as the word says. And if they do not want to change, the Holy Spirit himself will take care of removing them, because the church is the body of Christ, the pillar and foundation of Truth.

Living in the supernatural

When the church is able to live according to the principles God has established, rejecting all sin and hypocrisy, supernatural results will follow. The first result is believers multiplying. After Ananias and Sapphira died, the fear of God came upon the church, the Bible tells us: "More and more men and women believed in the Lord and were added to their number." People could have become frightened and started drifting away, but that was not what happened. They were amazed at what happened and the church began to grow, because where there is fear for the presence of God, there is life and growth.

The church grows because others want to be like us. We should attract other people to God. The presence of God in our lives is like a magnet, and that is why unbelievers seek us out whenever they have any kind of problem. This is what distinguishes a true Christian.

Other results were signs, wonders and miracles. All the sick in the surrounding villages were healed. Just Peter's shadow passing by was enough to heal the sick. I am praying for a powerful church, where people get saved and baptized immediately. The church must be committed to rescuing and caring for those who are added to it, because the moment they are saved, all of hell rises up against them. It is everyone's responsibility to see that they continue to move forward and progress in their newfound Christianity. In those days, three thousand people were saved and baptized on the same day. They did not have microphones or loudspeakers, or a baptistry, but nevertheless signs and wonders happened!

I have read about revivals all over the world. One of them began in a grocery store. The business owner was using pages from the Bible to wrap up his produce, and suddenly people started to read what was written and God began speaking to their hearts. There was an awakening in that city, and signs and wonders followed. We have everything we need in our hands today, but we do not value the benefits we have. For those who walk with God, even a rebuke is a blessing. Do not reject the fear of God or His reprimands.

Would you like to be part of the church today? Would you like to have the fear of God in your life and be a part of history in this time of change? We are the church of the living God and so many things are possible. We do not come to church only to seek our own blessing, but to have an encounter with One who blesses. We must be thirsty for God in order to remain in His House. Do not get accustomed to church; do not sit passively in the House of God. His House is a place of life! Do not let yourself get used to the Word, to the service, to coming together with your brothers and sisters, do not become a religious person.

Be sensitive to the Spirit of God, and allow Him to lead your life according to His principles. Where the Holy Spirit is, there is life and freedom, not death. I pray that you have the fear of the Lord and remain as a part of His redeeming church on earth, in spirit and in truth.

CHAPTER 5

I will not be apart

"And I tell you that you are Peter, and on this rock I will build my church, and the gates of Hades will not overcome it. I will give you the keys of the kingdom of heaven; whatever you bind on earth will be bound in heaven, and whatever you loose on earth will be loosed in heaven." Then he ordered his disciples not to tell anyone that he was the Messiah. …Peter took him aside and began to rebuke him. "Never, Lord!" he said. "This shall never happen to you!" Jesus turned and said to Peter, "Get behind me, Satan! You are a stumbling block to me; you do not have in mind the concerns of God, but merely human concerns."
Matthew 16:18-23

The central theme of this book is the House, by which I mean the church of the Living God. Thus far, I have presented different aspects of this House and what we should expect to find within it. I think it is important to reiterate that I am talking about us, the House of God, where the Most High dwells. The Bible says: "Do you not know that your bodies are temples of the Holy Spirit?" (1 Corinthians 6:19) We are the dwelling place of the Holy Spirit of God, and when we gather as the church of God, we become His House.

When I refer to the church, I do not want you to think of a powerful or well-known ministry. I am talking about the local church, which was planted by God to impact a specific area – that which expresses the purpose and the power of God in this time. The local church is not just a place to attend on Sundays; it is much more than that.

It is essential that we understand the importance of God's House, especially during a time when so many believers, who love God, are not planted in a local church. Whatever the reasons that led to their isolation, the fact is that every believer needs to be planted in a local church in order to be a part of God's plan in each region, and fully complete the Lord's plan for their life.

Many people have chosen to live an exclusively vertical Gospel – "just me and God" – they are this way because of disappointments or frustrations they've experienced in the body of Christ, through other believers or church leaders. We need to consider the wounds of our brothers and sisters, by caring for them and bringing them back to the "fold". The desire of my heart is to see each one of these people healed and involved in a church, loving the church and its leaders, because this will bring blessing without measure to the whole House.

As children of God, we know that we are constantly at war against the powers and principalities in the spiritual realm that intend to hinder the fulfillment of God's plans for our lives. Demons act strategically in the spiritual realm, attempting to confuse God's people concerning the importance of being planted in a local church. In this way, they paralyze God's House and weaken the body of Christ.

In Matthew 16:18-23, Jesus is in a special meeting with the disciples. By this time, they were already the church. They were learning wonderful things, and the presence of God manifested itself among them in an extraordinary way. On this occasion, Peter (the most restless and daring disciple, both in word and action) had a revelation from God. He had just answered a question from Jesus. If Peter were to be graded on his answer, he would have gotten an "A+"! When Jesus asked His disciples who they thought he was, Peter answered readily: "You are the Messiah, the Son of the living God" (Matthew 16:16). You could say that Peter "hit a home run." Jesus responded that Peter had received this revelation directly from the Father in Heaven. Right after, Jesus made a historic declaration saying: "And I tell you that you are Peter, and on this rock I will build my church, and the gates of Hades will not overcome it" (Matthew 16:18).

This is one of the most powerful passages in the Bible. It is the first time that Jesus Christ, the Son of the Living God, is being revealed, declared and manifested through the Holy Spirit of God, so much so that Jesus declares that the revelation had come from God Himself! God was present in that meeting. You may even think it was a small meeting due to the few people in attendance, but because of its potential in communicating God's plans, Jesus possibly could have already envisioned the great multitude gathered from around the world.

At that moment, the church was physically only twelve people, who were disciples of Jesus. I like to think that this was the very first Christian seminary, and the professor was Jesus Christ himself! What a privilege it was to attend that class!

Jesus told His disciples that the church would be given the keys to the Kingdom of God. He was delegating His authority to the church. Unfortunately, this is a stark contrast from the church today, which too often is passive, cowardly, mediocre and ignorant of its role in the world. The church received authority directly from Jesus Himself, and it cannot be a subdued and stagnant institution. For many years the devil has used the media to propagate this image of the church, day after day. Everything we see in the media concerning believers is derogatory, but I declare this is changing. We can see signs that the church is changing. But it is no good to merely change appearances or format. What the church desperately needs is an understanding of who we really are.

In the verse mentioned previously, Jesus said something tremendous. He made a powerful statement about the role of the church: it has the key to bind and to loose. But in the midst of this powerful meeting, and right after receiving this special revelation, Peter surprises us with his attitude. If earlier he had deserved an "A+", now all he would get was an "F". Perhaps he was feeling confident or superior after being praised by Jesus, but the fact is, Peter failed.

Yes, Peter failed soon after hitting the mark. Perhaps we would have made the same mistake. After all, we are human, just like Peter, and we have to be constantly alert in our walk with Jesus. Let's not forget that just because we have had a revelation, or because we have deep knowledge of the Bible, or because we are blessed, we can "take God's place" and say what we should do and how we should do it regarding God's purpose for the Lord Jesus. Peter is proof that receiving revelations from God does not exempt us from being used by the devil.

A believer may have revelations and be used by God, but the devil only needs a small opening to be able to use them as well. The devil has no respect for anyone – only for the blood of Jesus that is on our lives and the authority Jesus gave the church. If we give the devil an opportunity, God will not be free to save us from being used by him.

That's exactly what happened to Peter: he allowed an opening. I imagine that Peter, after being praised by Jesus and knowing that he had received a revelation "from God Himself, wow!", was full of himself, completely vain and proud. So while Peter was lost in his own thoughts, Jesus began to open His heart and share God's plan to the disciples. He told them about His fate in Jerusalem; He told of the suffering He would face and how he would die, but that after three days He would rise from the dead.

It's amazing how often our ears hear only what they want. Peter did not understand what Jesus was saying. Jesus said he would suffer and die, and that He would rise from the dead, but Peter only heard up to the "suffering and dying" point. We must learn to listen and discern the situations that surround us.

So Peter called Jesus, he "took him aside" (Matthew 16:22). What does this mean? At that special moment of profound revelations, Peter takes Jesus away from fellowship with other believers, away from where God was moving. Peter called Jesus apart from the body, removing Him from that environment of revelation, authority, openness of heart and sincerity. Jesus was opening His heart and sharing God's plan with His disciples. Just think how spectacular that meeting must have been! Something tremendous was happening in the church, and despite it all, Peter called Jesus aside.

The spirit that acted through Peter continues to operate in the same way today. I am not referring to Peter's spirit, but the spirit that used Peter's life. This spirit can use the life of anyone, If allowed an opportunity to remove us from the fellowship of the body. Do not be fooled, the church is not a place to go because it's "cool", nor because we like the way the services are done. This is not the perspective we should have of the church. You should be a part of the church because it is the expression of God on Earth; not a place for entertainment, but a place to experience the powerful presence of God. This is the right perspective! The church should be measured by the presence of God, by the content of the word, by holiness, by the search for God, by correct doctrine, and above all, by knowing God has planted us in this place to help us grow and bear fruit. This is the church.

It seems that the latest trend is to belong to the "Church of Christ", but not be connected to any local church. Believers should enjoy belonging to a local church, and contributing their gifts to

THE HOUSE | WELCOME HOME!

the church; we have to understand that it is at the local church that we fulfill our calling and ministry, according to God's will. We should enjoy serving in the church of the living God.

Remember that Jesus was in fellowship with the church when Peter called him aside. Fellowship is very important in the House of God; it helps reveal our shortcomings. Some people do not like to be with "other people", but it is fundamental. It is through our relationships that we discover some of our weak points; it is through contact with others that we discover who we truly are. For example, you might find that you are unsympathetic when relating to others, and from that awareness take the opportunity to change. The greatest virtue and quality of being a believer is not perfection, but having the privilege to change through the Holy Spirit. Change is a blessing. If you don't change, you will crumble and self destruct.

There is a spirit that wants to separate us from what God wants for us, separate us from God's calling and God's will. Peter was taking Jesus away from God's will. It was necessary that Jesus suffer, die and, on the third day, rise again so we could receive salvation. He had to go through all of this to take the keys of hell and death from the hands of the devil. Jesus was not going to die just to become one more martyr; He went through all of that so that with His blood he could pay every penny of the debt we owed. And after he paid it, Jesus canceled all our written debt, so that there would be no memory of our past.

Peter's mistake was not only trying to interfere with what Jesus must suffer, but even worse, it was removing Him from fellowship. He called Jesus aside: aside from the believers, the people, the fellowship of the body of Christ, where we hear and speak. This is exactly what the devil does; he isolates us so we can only hear his voice, and no longer hear our Father's.

A classic example is what the devil did to Eve. The serpent spoke directly to Eve while she was away from Adam. He waited for an opportunity when Eve would be alone and isolated, to tell her something that God did not say! The serpent lured Eve away from Adam's protection. If Adam had been nearby, they probably would have argued over what God had said and it would not have been that easy to fool them.

Peter was being used by the devil to call Jesus aside, to try and distract Him from His commitment, from the covenant and the responsibilities He faced at the time. If Peter had taken him further away, it would have been easier to instill doubts about what God had said. This is a common strategy used by the enemy, and if Jesus had to face it, we will too.

The devil does not joke around. He knows when we are isolated and become easy prey for his attacks. This is why he fights to have people who love God stray from the church and remain isolated in their own thoughts. This happened to Jesus and it is written in the Bible as an example for all of us. Do not allow anything to separate you from the Body, to separate you from what God has for you.

The church is a place of commitment, of covenant. The simple act of belonging to a church, of being connected to your local church, has great value in the spiritual world. The Bible says that we are the body of Christ:

> *And God placed all things under his feet and appointed him to be head over everything for the church, which is his body, the fullness of him who fills everything in every way.*
> Ephesians 1:22-23

> *For just as each of us has one body with many members, and these members do not all have the same function, so in Christ we, though many, form one body, and each member belongs to all the others. We have different gifts, according to the grace given to each of us. If your gift is prophesying, then prophesy in accordance with your faith; if it is serving, then serve; if it is teaching, then teach; if it is to encourage, then give encouragement; if it is giving, then give generously; if it is to lead do it diligently; if it is to show mercy, do it cheerfully.*
> Romans 12:4-8

Each of us has a role in God's House. We cannot be a church if we have no commitment, or do not submit to authority, especially since even in society, well-organized groups are divided. None of us can live alone. The church should be an example of authority (that binds and looses), where not even the gates of Hades will prevail – but will be destroyed by a powerful church living in commitment and covenant with God and each other.

Commitment is a key to blessings in our lives. Whoever is committed to school is blessed; whoever is committed to work is blessed. Commitment is linked to the Kingdom of God and His word, so we must make the commitment and fight to keep it. The church is blessed because it has a commitment to the word. When the word is preached, the Holy Spirit speaks to every heart according to each person's needs. This mystery holds true for all of us, from new converts to renowned pastors. When the word of God is released, no one is left out, no matter how mature or new a believer may be, He speaks to everyone.

The word of God is living. It is not a list of forbidden things or rules we memorize to find peace. The Bible is not a good luck charm, nor a book that defeats our enemies. The power to defeat our enemies is in the word of God when it is declared and exercised with authority. In other words, the words of the Bible have to be lived through us.

If we study Peter's attitude, we will see that he was acting outside the Body. Why not question Jesus' fate together with the other disciples? If Peter had been guided by the Holy Spirit, there would have been agreement in the rest of the Body. However, when Peter called Jesus aside, he was trying to change God's plan for His life. When he moved away from the body, Peter provided an opportunity for the devil to use him to seriously interfere with God's plan.

The battles waged in the spiritual world are serious and real. When a believer is not spiritually aligned with Christ, they are placing themselves in great danger, no matter if they are new believers or an experienced believer.

Do not be isolated; do not stay outside God's House. It is in church that you will discover God's plan for your life, and where you will flourish. Whether you are a new or seasoned believer, pray that God provides you the understanding and wisdom to see that even if we do not understand everything, we must remain where He has planted us.

CHAPTER 6
The House: Where you have to believe it to see it

On the evening of that first day of the week, when the disciples were together, with the doors locked for fear of the Jewish leaders, Jesus came and stood among them and said, "Peace be with you!" After he said this, he showed them his hands and side. The disciples were overjoyed when they saw the Lord. Again Jesus said, "Peace be with you! As the Father has sent me, I am sending you." And with that he breathed on them and said, "Receive the Holy Spirit. If you forgive anyone's sins, their sins are forgiven; if you do not forgive them, they are not forgiven."

Now Thomas (also known as Didymus), one of the Twelve, was not with the disciples when Jesus came. So the other disciples told him, "We have seen the Lord!" But he said to them, "Unless I see the nail marks in his hands and put my finger where the nails were, and put my hand into his side, I will not believe." A week later his disciples were in the house again, and Thomas was with them. Though the doors were locked, Jesus came and stood among them and said, "Peace be with you!" Then he said to Thomas, "Put your finger here; see my hands. Reach out your hand and put it into my side. Stop doubting and believe." Thomas said to him, "My Lord and my God!" Then Jesus told him, "Because you have seen me, you have believed; blessed are those who have not seen and yet have believed."

John 20:19-29

Have you ever been in such an incredible situation, that when you told the story to your friends, they said: "I'd have to see it, to believe it!?" In the House of God, the opposite is true: You have to believe it, to see it. There is a character in the Bible who used this common expression in different words. His name was Thomas. He said: "Unless I see the nail marks in his hands and put my finger where the nails were, and put my hand into his side, I will not believe." In other words, Thomas was saying: "I'd have to see it, to believe it." Due to Thomas' unbelief, Jesus teaches us a vital lesson for the Christian life: first, we must believe. "And these signs will accompany those who believe (Mark 16:17)."

After Jesus' death on the cross, the disciples were meeting behind closed doors, out of fear for what the Jews might be thinking: If they did that to Jesus, what will they do to us? We had better stay out of sight. Suddenly, Jesus appeared among them, saying "Peace be with you." Remember that the Church is a place where people gather for Jesus Christ. The disciples were meeting together in that house, even though they were afraid and insecure. They were waiting that something would happen. And all of a sudden, without opening any doors, Jesus appears in their midst, resurrected.

Later, the disciples told Thomas their encounter with Jesus, since he had not been at the meeting. We could say that Thomas "missed church" that day, and missed a historic and supernatural moment that the other disciples experienced. I can imagine that Thomas was unaware of the recent events and his faith had begun to weaken, because he was not with his brothers in the House. As he drifted away from fellowship with his brothers, unbelief had begun to fill the heart of a man who had seen Jesus perform miracles and wonders.

THE HOUSE | WELCOME HOME!

In John 20:26, it says that Thomas spent a week away, held captive by unbelief: "A week later His disciples were in the house again, and Thomas was with them." He had to wait a week for the next meeting, and he was not going to miss it this time!

One meeting can make all the difference in our lives, because in every service Jesus is there, speaking to us, touching our lives and hearts with his word. Be careful, because if you miss a meeting, you may become out of touch with what God is doing through His Gospel, the Good News, the Gospel. We need to value God's House and delight in being there. We need to learn from David: I rejoiced with those who said to me, "Let us go to the house of the Lord" (Psalms 122:1).

Given the increasing number of "churches" today, many believers do not value the House of God. There are many options: church on the radio, church on television, church on the internet… But we must not confuse the messages we hear from these sources with the church. Being part of the church is sitting in church, next to your brothers; it is a covenant with the leaders of the church; it is receiving spiritual food and beginning to bear fruit; church is loving your brothers and having fellowship with them. When we are together, Jesus is in our midst. That is a promise from the Lord.

As in our daily lives, Jesus appeared to the disciples at a time when they were very sad and scared. They doubted if Jesus had really risen from the dead. But the Master suddenly appeared and showed the disciples the scars in His hands and in His side (where the soldier had pierced Him) to prove that it was really Him and remove any doubt. The Bible tells us that everyone was full of joy. It was an incredible meeting! Jesus breathed the Holy Spirit on them and told them many things.

Thomas, who had not been present and had missed the move of God, wanted to experience for himself what the other disciples had experienced. But that was not possible. You cannot reproduce what occurs in each worship service. If you want to hear what God has to say to you today, be at the meeting and pay attention. God has something new for you every day. His promises and His Words are endless. Thomas wanted to go back in time, he wanted to see it to believe it…but the Bible tells us to believe first if we want to see it.

When Thomas came to the second meeting, despite his unbelief, things still happened! Jesus appeared to him too. If the disciples were able to convince doubting Thomas to come to the second meeting, you should also try to bring a person who does not know Jesus, so that Jesus can reveal Himself to them as well. Do not be afraid to bring an unbeliever to church, because the Lord who revealed Himself to Thomas is among us today as well. Beware of the spirit that tries to take us out of the church and fellowship. As we saw in the previous chapter, Jesus was meeting with His disciples, with His church, when Peter called Him aside and removed Him from fellowship. Jesus was in the church, in fellowship with His brothers and needed to share His heart.

This reminds us that the church is not only a place of victory. Sometimes, you can be in church feeling sad, but your sadness disappears with a hug from a brother or sister, an encouraging word and the presence of Jesus Christ. The church is also a place of trust, to share and receive comfort. Jesus told His disciples that He would suffer and die in Jerusalem, but that He would rise from the dead on the third day. Peter calls Him aside and advises Him to have mercy on Himself. Jesus' reaction was not treating Peter with gentleness and love. At that moment, Jesus does not even respond to Peter, but to the spirit that was influencing him. Jesus said, "Get behind me, Satan!" Peter took Jesus out of Church, from his relationships, from the moment of opening and sharing His heart and from fellowship. This is what the devil does. Never let anything take you away from fellowship. Anything that takes you away from the purposes of God is called Satan, even when there is good intentions.

We learned from the examples of Thomas and Peter that the spirit of deception does not manifest itself in the church, but operates outside of it. When we are in church, we are in the light. If Peter had spoken to Jesus in front of the other disciples, he may have been reprimanded by one of the brothers. But the spirit of deception can only manifest itself outside of fellowship. That is why Peter called Jesus aside from the others.

Everything that Jesus does is an example for us. When Peter took Jesus outside of fellowship, the Master showed His authority saying: "Get behind me, Satan!" (Matthew 16:23) We need to be prepared for when the spirit of deception tries to deceive us when we are outside the church. We can overcome with the authority in the name of Jesus. Jesus' example is extraordinary. He replied at the right time, with the right answer. Let's imagine the scene of that meeting: Peter, with an arrogant air, and calling Jesus aside; then, Peter walking back with Jesus, with his head down. Going back to the example of Thomas, we see that Jesus returned to their second meeting, but Thomas was with them. This time Thomas was prepared not to miss service. And, to his joy and comfort, Jesus appeared to them again! So, how did Jesus solve Thomas' problem? In John 20:27, He says to His doubting disciple: "Put your finger here; see my hands. Reach out your hand and put it into my side. Stop doubting and believe."

When God manifests during a meeting, He touches the most needy people there. God knew the condition of Thomas' heart: tormented, in doubt and disbelief. Why did Jesus tell Thomas to touch His wounds? Firstly, because that is what Thomas wanted most. When Jesus told Thomas to put his hand on the wounds in His hands and side, He was teaching us a lesson. Jesus was saying to Thomas: "Touch my body".

How can we touch Jesus' body today? When we touch the church, this is exactly what we are doing: we are touching the body of Christ. When you're in church, it is as if you are touching Jesus because His presence is there. If there is someone doubting in the church, something is going to happen. According to Ephesians 1:22-23, the church is the body of Christ. Whoever touches the body of Christ, touches the church. Did Thomas actually touch Jesus? No. In fact, he did not actually touch Him. The scales fell from his eyes before that. Let's read verses 27 and 28: Then he said to Thomas, "Put your finger here; see my hands. Reach out your hand and put it into my side. Stop doubting and believe." Thomas said to him, "My Lord and my God!" The words Jesus spoke were enough to cause the scales to fall and to cast out the spirit of deception in Thomas' life. Why? Because Thomas was now in the body.

The church is much more than a meeting where believers worship. The church is a gathering where we represent the Body of Jesus on Earth. The authority of Jesus is in the church. It is in the church that we adore and worship God Almighty. The church is the living body of Jesus.
How many things prevent you from being planted in the church? Satan uses subtle and strategic situations to try and take us away from the body, because he knows that when you are in church, your life is transformed.

Why do we need to touch the body of Christ? Because when we are a part of the body of Christ, all our doubt and unbelief disappears, because in fellowship, there is the presence of God and the revelation of His Word. Our paths are lit and we can clearly see where we should walk: Your word is a lamp for my feet, a light to my path. (Psalms 119:105) When we are in the body, the House of God, the word we receive lights our way and prevents us from stumbling.

Thomas stopped doubting and began to believe much more than he did before. When did he begin to believe? When did the scales fall off his eyes? In the church. The presence of Jesus melts away all doubt and casts out all fears. The spirit of deception and unbelief are broken in fellowship.

Besides, the church is also a place of change. You can change. Abraham changed, even though he was over 100 years old! His wife Sarah had a baby at almost 90 years old. Caleb was 85 when he went to battle to conquer the Promised Land. Let others be surprised by the change in your life! It is never too late to change.

We are living in days when God is restoring power to the church, its beauty and effectiveness. Any opposition that comes against the church will fall; it will be a place of spontaneity and freedom, a place for the presence of God and celebrations full of beauty and emotion. The church is where we show the world that Christ is in us, the Hope of Glory!

Come Home! Be planted in the body. Outside of it, there is no way to take part in the God's plan for humanity. "For the creation waits in eager expectation for the children of God to be revealed." (Romans 8:19). The manifestation of the power and glory of God, that's what is happening in us – in the unity of God's House.

CHAPTER 7
HOME: Prepare for the new

MARCO A. PEIXOTO

After the death of Moses the servant of the Lord, the Lord said to Joshua son of Nun, Moses' aide: "Moses my servant is dead. Now then, you and all these people, get ready to cross the Jordan River into the land I am about to give to them—to the Israelites. I will give you every place where you set your foot, as I promised Moses."
Joshua 1:1-3

Anything new requires change. You cannot receive something new in your life without making room for it, without changing your daily routine, without something being required of you. Be it a new job, a new house, the arrival of a baby into the family: nothing new can happen without action that brings change. And everything new, even if it involves happiness, generates or creates expectation and some fear. How will things be from now on?

During the years in the wilderness, the people of Israel experienced big changes. One of the greatest changes was the death of their leader, Moses, and the emergence of a new leader, Joshua. And even Joshua himself experienced a huge change in his life: he would no longer be a servant of Moses, but would be the leader in his place. Certainly Joshua must have thought: How will things be from now on?

In Joshua, Chapter 1, verses 1-3, God exhorts Joshua regarding his new position. He says to the young leader that there is a necessary requirement that he should possess. Joshua needed this requirement to conquer the land of Canaan, his inheritance. God uses different words to communicate His message to Joshua, highlighting the importance of this requirement so that he could take possession of what God had promised him already.

When the Book of Joshua begins, Moses, the great leader was dead. Joshua knew that already. And all the people knew as well. But, God begins His message to Joshua by saying: "Moses my servant is dead" (Joshua 1:1). We may not understand exactly why God was emphasizing the death of Moses, after all, Joshua already knew. However, let's reflect on the words of the Lord, because nothing He says is without purpose. By emphasizing a known fact, God is insisting that Joshua understand something very important and key for his new journey: he needed to bury the past. God was advising him, as if saying: Moses is dead, it's over! Bury the past, forget it. Move forward, go ahead! No one can move forward into the future while looking into the rearview mirror of the past.

There is great power and wisdom in the words of the Lord to Joshua, and they were fundamental in that moment. Of course, Joshua could have remained idle in the past, remembering the glorious moments beside a great servant of the Lord. However, God knows that whoever lives idly in the past cannot take possession of the future. To live idly in the past is a curse. Whenever we preserve the past, in a way we are running from the future. When we preserve the past, we are basically living a life that is outdated. If today becomes yesterday, there are no expectations for tomorrow. Stop and think about it a little; I'm sure you know people like that. They live in the glories of their past every day and never envision the possibilities that tomorrow may bring.

THE HOUSE | WELCOME HOME!

Just when he was getting ready to enter the Promised Land, Joshua received hard instructions from the Lord. In other words, God told him: "Joshua, Moses died. But the promise I made to him, you will fulfill. Everything I promised will happen. Go ahead. Do not act within the confines of what happened with Moses. This is a new time and I will act through you. Do not cling to the past. Depend on Me (God) for the future."

Joshua did not respond. His lips did not move, but we can imagine what he was thinking. What would you or I be thinking if we were in his place? God was able to do such great things through Moses and now Moses is dead. Who am I? Will I be able to lead this people? So many things have already happened! Moses faced so many things during his life, and even got tired and disappointed, what about me? Will I be able to lead this people? Like Joshua, many of us keep memories that oppress us and basically paralyze us. Even though our lips do not admit it, our thoughts frighten and paralyze us. How will things be from now on?

The Scriptures say that there is great power in our thoughts. Proverbs 23:7 says: "For as he thinks within himself, so he is." In other words, our thoughts are able to shape our actions. And that's why God did not want Joshua to have any thoughts in his mind that could paralyze him, because if he did he would not be able to envision the future. By clinging to memories of the past, Joshua would be unable to enter and take possession of his thoughts. Therefore, Joshua would have never fulfilled the plan God had for his life.

I want to remember that which gives hope. Wanting something is a personal decision; I have to want it. I want memories that give me hope. There are some memories that kill. There are people who only use their memories to be depressed. They have memories that destroy their sense of humor or mood, their life, and their hope. Feed your mind with hope, feed your mind with the Word of God and remember: "Everything is possible for those who believe."

After reiterating the death of Moses, God is even more emphatic concerning the necessity to leave the past behind. He said: "Arise now!" (Joshua 1:2). It is only possible to arise now to take possession now, when you are free from the things of the past. Some people live constantly based upon facts that have already passed. They never tire of repeating their glories or disappointments that happened in the past:

"It's in the past!"
"Oh, but it hurt's…"
"It's in the past!"
"Oh, but it was so painful!"
"It's in the past!"
"Oh, but I remember it as if it happened yesterday…"

When we make room for statements like these, we allow the spirit of helplessness, that spirit that

MARCO A. PEIXOTO

wants to make us retreat, that wants to prevent us from moving forward and experiencing new things. Although it may seem hard, this message from the Lord must be received by each of us. He told Joshua to move forward: Leave your past. Get ready now! Your promise of a future life has arrived! Forget what Moses experienced and what you saw. I am going to do something new now! Take your eyes off Moses. This is a different time. You are going to enter the land. And He is telling you too: It does not matter how hurt or disappointed you are. It does not matter what was left behind, or what is dead. What matters is what is alive and waiting for you. There are new things in your path waiting for you. Move forward. Take hold of them.

We serve a God that is moving, and we must do the same. In verse 3, the Lord continues, saying to Joshua: "I will give you every place where you set your foot, as I promised Moses." God always calls us to advance and to conquer using our own two feet. So, there's no use in just standing there, afraid of the new. We need to move toward the new things God has for us. Besides the personal application to every believer in Jesus, the words of the Lord to Joshua are a lesson for the Church today, as well. Satan has used numerous situations to stop us or keep us in the past. He makes us think: I already tried…It will never happen again. I am too hurt and weary. These are not the kind of thoughts we should hold onto, on the contrary, we should be determined to try again, even if it wear us out again! Believe for the new again! Move forward. You are living a new day.

Jesus said to Peter: "Go into the deep seas." Jesus sent Peter back to the place of frustration. And, although he had fished the whole night and caught nothing, Jesus made him go back to the same place during the day, and he filled the boat with so many fish to the point that it was going to sink. And, so with Jesus; you can go back and do things that you had given up on in the past.

That was the mentality, the kind of thinking that God wanted to instill in Joshua, the mentality of a "new day" and "possession." This was Joshua's moment, and Satan knew it. Thoughts like: If he could not posses it, will I posses it? If he didn't do it, will I be able to do it?, If he couldn't, can I?, invade the minds of Christians in order to make us stop. Do not permit Satan to stop you from pursuing and achieving the new things God has for your life and for His Kingdom.

Another important step relating to the "moving forward" mentality is our tendency or need to cling to people: mother, father, leaders. Everyone mourned the death of Moses and it would be normal for Joshua to feel alone, with no direction, wondering how Moses would solve the questions he faced. He had such wisdom, and was patient. But God prepared Joshua by telling him: Moses is dead. Arise now. You will enter the Promised Land. This is a strong message of preparation, because Joshua had to break free from Moses to pursue his own way. So, do not worry about the experiences of others, their failures, or let their negative feelings contaminate you and cause you to become negative or absent. The past is dead, and God is preparing you for the new!

Besides Joshua, other biblical characters were prisoners to the death of others and were exhorted by God. The Bible tells us about two disciples who had left Jerusalem and were on the road to Emmaus (about 14 or 15 miles away), after the crucifixion of Jesus. They were walking and talking when Jesus appeared amongst them, but they could not recognize Him. Their minds were fixed on the fact that Jesus had died and therefore, they did not recognize that He was with them. They were stuck in the past! Even though only three days had lapsed, the past is the past. Yesterday is not today. Jesus had died, resurrected, and was right there with them. Why weren't they celebrating His resurrection? Because they were blinded by the past.

In Luke 24:17-21, Jesus asks these two disciples: "What are you discussing together as you walk along?" And they stopped, grieving, and answered, "Are you the only one visiting Jerusalem who does not know the things that have happened there in these days? About Jesus of Nazareth. He was a prophet, powerful in word and deed before God and all the people. The chief priests and our rulers handed him over to be sentenced to death, and they crucified him; but we had hoped that he was the one who was going to redeem Israel. And what is more, it is the third day since all this took place." Their response clearly shows that these two disciples were stuck in the past. When you are bound to the past, you do not recognize the present and see nothing for the future. By not recognizing the risen Christ, the two disciples were not ready to receive His promise. The fact that these disciples were right next to Jesus and did not recognize Him is a warning for us about the danger of the past. Don't be stuck in the past; prepare for the new! Believe that new things will come to your house, your ministry and your job, because new things are on the way for your future! Choose to believe and think about the future again. In Lamentations 3:21, the prophet Jeremiah says: "Yet this I call to mind and therefore I have hope." He chooses to stop thinking about the past and hope for something better. In verse 20 he is remembering bad and negative things: "I well remember them, and my soul is downcast within me." Meaning that not only was this a reminder of the past, he was continuously remembering and this discouraged him.

When the two disciples were walking toward Emmaus, they were downcast because they were stuck in the past, remembering Jesus' crucifixion and death. Jesus, however, was right next to them, resurrected, the Almighty, ready to do things never seen before. But they ignored Him.
There is a fundamental principle we need to understand: God cannot reveal Himself in our lives when we are stuck continually burying things in the past, looking at things that have already died. The death of Jesus was a fact: He died and was buried, but He is no longer dead! He is risen! We are living the Gospel of the risen Christ! When Mary went to the tomb, asking who had stolen the body of the Lord, the angels replied: "Why do you look for the living among the dead?" (see Luke 24:5). Not even the death of Jesus can be a symbol of paralysis for us.

As soon as I got saved, I observed people partaking of the Lord's Supper and thought it must be a sad moment, because I saw so many people crying. Before I was baptized and could partake as well, I was looking for reasons to cry and be sad in that moment, because I thought it was the right thing to do. Fortunately, I soon discovered that the Lord's Supper is not a time of sadness. It is a reminder filled with rejoicing, joy and gladness, because He rose and freed us from sin, from the past and from hell!

MARCO A. PEIXOTO

Satan works with the goal of keeping our minds in the past, but we must follow the Word of God, which says: "Forgetting what is behind and straining toward what is ahead" (Philippines 3:13). The choice is yours. It's up to you to choose what you remember: things that give hope, as the prophet Jeremiah did, or things that discourage and oppress. Do not ask God to choose for you, because this is your personal responsibility. It is you who must choose between the memories that build or that destroy.

Do you know how Jesus "refreshed" the memory of the two disciples walking to Emmaus? The Bible says that He, "beginning with Moses and all the Prophets, explained to them what was said in all the Scriptures concerning himself" (Luke 24:27). Jesus preached to them the Word, making references to the passages that spoke about Him. By doing so, He was trying to tell them the following: I am not dead, I am risen. Did you think the grave could hold me? My Father, God Almighty, has already freed me. I have conquered death and risen. Jesus was preaching so that their minds would change. The disciples' wanted to remember only the bad; they were worried about themselves, were afraid of being killed. Our minds begin to lose touch with reality when we are fixated on the past. This hinders our present and future. Jesus was preparing the two disciples to receive what God had prepared for them in the future. Likewise, God was preparing Joshua for what had been intended for him later.

You may have past memories, but you can't live dependent on them. You are free to pursue and take what God has prepared for your life, for your home, for your family. You can live in all the promises of God, as long as you choose to free yourself from thoughts of death and embrace the life and the future God has for you. That is the Word of God for your future!

CHAPTER 8
Only sleeping

When Jesus returned, a crowd was waiting to welcome Him, for they were all expecting His visit. So a man named Jairus, a synagogue leader, came and fell at Jesus' feet, pleading with him to come to his house because his only daughter, a girl of about twelve, was dying... But he took her by the hand and said, "My child, get up!"... Her parents were astonished, but he ordered them not to tell anyone what had happened.

Luke 8:40-56

While on earth Jesus had the opportunity to live among people of great public authority. In Luke, chapter 8, the Bible introduces a man named Jairus, who was the leader of the Synagogue. When reading the passage, we can imagine that Jairus was a religious leader of his time, but history tells us that during Jesus' life, this position was the equivalent of a mayor or something similar. Jairus was the single leader responsible for the synagogue in that city, and this was a great responsibility. Therefore, Jairus was a well-known man, with much power and authority, apart from also being a rich man. He had everything: reputation, honor, power, wealth. Who wouldn't want to visit his home? Jairus probably lived in a large, comfortable and beautiful house, but inside its walls was a spirit of death. Despite all his power and authority, Jairus had no power over death, which was about to take his twelve year-old daughter. The girl had been sick for a long time, and now was dying.

Let's take a look at the attitude of this man. Luke, chapter 8, verse 41 says: "Then a man named Jairus, a synagogue leader, came and fell at Jesus' feet, pleading with him to come to his house." The first thing about his attitude that grabs our attention is: instead of wishing Jesus would come to his house, Jairus first leaves his house to go find Jesus. He left that environment; he left his dying daughter and went to meet Jesus, the King of kings and Lord of lords. Secondly, Jairus made the most important decision of his life: when he met Jesus, he fell at His feet. This is the attitude of a man who wants to find perfect wisdom. He realized that all he had, and all that he was, meant nothing! The most dangerous thing that keeps us away from God is not the devil, but ourselves, when we do not understand that nothing can be more valuable than Jesus.

Religion, power, fame, charisma or wealth did not stop Jairus from leaving everything behind and falling on the ground, pleading: Lord, my daughter is dying; help me. Lord, can you come to my house? There is nothing else left to do, but I know that You are Lord and You can perform a miracle in my daughter's life. Come to my house with me!

Jairus, the great leader, left us a great lesson. Many people only want Jesus to come to them, but never go to Him, let alone humble themselves to receive Him. Many people have status, wealth, knowledge and fame, but until we leave all these things behind and fall at the feet of the Fountain of wisdom and life, we will be left with nothing except for the things we have acquired – and even those vanish quickly. Blessed are those who recognize that they are nothing, and everything they have is nothing compared to Christ and consequently bow down before the King of kings. They will receive abundant and eternal life!

THE HOUSE | WELCOME HOME!

Are you willing to wait for Jesus? In a society characterized by an "instant" mentality, how many of us know how to wait for God's timing? While Jairus waited patiently for Jesus to come with him, many things happened. On the way, a woman touched Jesus. He stopped, the disciples stopped, and the crowd stopped. Jesus wanted to know who in the crowd had touched Him: "Someone has touched me; I know that power has gone out from me" (Luke 8:46). Meanwhile, the leader of the synagogue was watching, waiting with great anticipation for Jesus to come to his house to heal his daughter. He did not "rush" Jesus, like many of us do when we are waiting for an answer to our needs. What other feeling, apart from full trust in Jesus, would make a father wait for Him? At that moment, a voice came from his house, saying: "Your daughter is dead. Don't bother the Master anymore" (Luke 8:49).

Imagine yourself in Jairus' place, waiting for Jesus. What kind of thoughts must have gone through his mind? Jesus took too long, my daughter has died. Perhaps, if He hadn't stopped… Jairus had lost a daughter, and was experiencing a different, unexpected moment in his life.

This passage in Luke 8 not only portrays the story of Jairus; it also portrays our lives. We have given up on many things because we heard a voice tells us: It's over. There is nothing left to do. Give up! It's impossible! You tried, but failed. This is the voice of intimidation that confronts us and leaves us weary and paralyzed. "Your daughter is dead." Death is the absence of life and opportunity. Many things happen in our lives very subtly, in order to rob us of the opportunities we have to experience bigger things. We are waiting for Jesus, but when He seems to take longer than we'd like, the voice of intimidation tries to make us give up. Like what happened to Jairus, voices can whisper in your ear to try to make you give up and leave what is dead behind. Jesus, however, will awaken things in you that you believed were dead. When Jesus arrived at Jairus' house, he spoke to those who were mourning for the girl: "Stop wailing. She is not dead but asleep" (Luke 8:52). The things we thought were "dead" are only "asleep"; and will be awakened by the supernatural power of God.

Like Jairus, we are tested as we wait for the Lord. Our faith will be subjected to the voices of discouragement and giving up, but it will also be strengthened by the voice of hope. In this Biblical story, we can observe two voices. The first said "Your daughter is dead." But the second voice said "Don't be afraid. Just believe." The first voice is one of fear, that says: "it is over", but on the other hand, the voice of hope says: "believe". And this happens in our lives as well. There will always be two voices, that of faith and of fear.

Jairus had to choose what voice to trust. Imagine the conflict in his mind the moment he received news that his daughter had died. He could have chosen the voice of despair and become paralyzed; he could have let panic take over his life to the point of not hearing the voice of Jesus. The Bible has other examples that are similar to the situation Jairus experienced, that any of us might experience. No circumstance or problem is bigger than another; but different people react differently to the same situation. And the devil knows very well how to torment us. However, regardless of what the voice of the devil tells you, choose to hear and believe the voice of Jesus: "Believe. It is possible." Don't believe the voices that come straight from hell, that release fear in your heart, and rob you of the word of God. These tormenting voices leave us paralyzed to the point that we can only see the circumstances we are facing and nothing more than that. The devil had prepared a future of torment for Jairus, but the Lord changed the story.

When He was on the cross, Jesus also faced those tormenting voices. Despite being the Son of God, those were not easy moments for Jesus; He was divine, but also human, and as a man, He faced those tormenting voices until the very end. Hanging on the cross, Jesus heard: "Come down from the cross, if you are the Son of God! He saved others, but he can't save himself!" There are times when we have to choose between what God has told us to do and what we want to do. Jesus had to hold on to His Father's word. While those men mocked him, the human side of Jesus could have thought of destroying them with a single word, but He kept quiet, he suffered quietly because of His love for us, and above all, because He was obedient to the Father. Jesus paid no attention to those voices because he could see the future.

When Jairus heard the news about his daughter, he could have fallen into despair, and let his faith in Jesus wither. Faith or despair? "Simply believe; have no fear" or "Your daughter is dead". Which voice should Jairus believe? Which voice should Jairus obey: the voice of the Lord, or the voice that brought the message of death? We need to understand that we are responsible to actively respond to God. He will never obey for us. God will never do for you what you can do yourself. God was not obedient for Jesus, but Jesus obeyed God. There are blessings in the Word of God, but we have to believe and obey. When you believe in the word of God, He will do things for you that you cannot do.

Jairus chose to continue trusting and waiting for Jesus, and when Christ finally arrived at his home, he said "Stop wailing. She is not dead but asleep" (Luke 8:52). Although everything may point towards death, if Jesus says that the things in your life are not dead but asleep, believe Him! You may think that something is finished or dead, but Jesus has the power to awaken it.

Upon arriving at Jairus' home, Jesus took two important actions regarding the surrounding circumstances. We need to analyze both actions and apply these principles to our own lives.
First of all, Jesus sent out all who doubted. The people in Jairus' house who doubted Him were unbelievers who thought Jesus could only help the living. They did not know that the one who had arrived was the Author of Life Himself.

Secondly, He called to those who believed to come inside – those whom He could count on. Jesus was preparing an explosion of power and miracles, so He called three of His disciples to see something extraordinary! It was the first time that Peter, James and John were called to participate in something supernatural. They witnessed something powerful! They were chosen from the twelve because they believed and were open to learning. Later, the Bible tells us that Peter used the same words that Jesus used to resurrect Jairus' daughter to resurrect a disciple in Acts, chapter 9, verse 40.

THE HOUSE | WELCOME HOME!

Learn from Jesus, and set aside those who do not contribute to your spiritual life. Do not walk with people who weaken your faith. Of course, you should not reject such people, but you should not join them. Walk with people who will help you get where you want to go, and not with people who take you in the opposite direction. As in the past, God wants to perform extraordinary works in this day and time, but only for those who are close by, tasting and seeing, those who believe and walk with Jesus. Are you close enough to Him to participate and be impacted by miracles? Do not be a bystander! Do not draw close just to see Jesus, but to receive the power and virtue of the Holy Spirit. These things cannot be missing in the life of a Christian.

Besides the disciples, Peter, James and John, Jesus also called for the mother and father of the girl. Jairus was already with Jesus, but He also called for the mother, in order to emphasize the principle of family unity. God desires to see our families united, honoring and excited about spiritual things. He desires to see a family filled with miracles and participating together in God's work. The mother and father of the little girl needed a miracle. The girl did not need a miracle, because she was already dead. She became the miracle.

By bringing her back to life, Jesus teaches us that when people with a need unite with people who believe, miracles can happen. There must be a link between need and faith. Do not settle for things that have fallen "asleep" in your life, such as: "This is how I'm going to talk, and this is how I'm going to act." Change your habits! Only death robs us of the opportunity. Are you alive? Then there is a miracle waiting to happen in your life.

At the end of the Biblical story, Jesus extends his hand and performs the miracle: He took her by the hand and said "My child, get up!" (Luke 8:54) It is not in your hand; it is the hand of the Lord that works the impossible and raises up what is asleep. The hand of the Lord is able to raise what has fallen, and He will lift you up to a new day. Bad news will not kill the things that are asleep in your life. Believe, and He will awaken what is asleep in your life.

Jesus said: "give her something to eat". The girl who was resurrected was hungry and needed something to eat. Those who are alive have appetites. Not only should we have an appetite for natural food; but for an abundant life filled with the presence of Jesus Christ!